INSTANT NEGOTIATOR™

THE COMPLETE GUIDE TO BUILDING WEALTH AND CREATING HAPPINESS

Frank D'Alessandro

AMERICAN NEGOTIATION INSTITUTE

First Edition

Production Manager: Todd P. Fitzgerald

Production Design: Rosanne Gauthier

Back Cover Photo: Inspired Images

Library of Congress Card Number: 00-101588

ISBN 1-930307-00-4

TRADEMARKS

The following are trademarks of Instant Negotiator, Inc.: INSTANT NEGOTIATOR, WHAT YOU ACHIEVE IN LIFE IS IN DIRECT PROPORTION TO HOW WELL YOU NEGOTIATE, CONTROL YOUR DESTINY and THE GUIDING TRAFFIC SIGN MEMORY SYSTEM & DESIGN.

This book is dedicated to my grandmother
Yvonne DeFina
whose selfless love and nurturing gave
me the strength to find my way in life.

Tell us your best negotiation story and we may print it in the next INSTANT NEGOTIATOR™ book!

Everyone has at least one business or personal negotiation story that stands out. The American Negotiation Institute (ANI) is collecting interesting, even humorous negotiation stories for a new book in the works. If you have a great story to tell, contact ANI via mail or e-mail:

Mailing Address:
8801 College Parkway # 1, Ft. Myers, FL 33919

E-Mail:
Frank@AmericanNegotiationInstitute.com

CONTENTS

Page

CHAPTER THREE

The INSTANT NEGOTIATOR Style

CHAPTER FOUR

Step 1: Know Your Opponent

CHAPTER NINE

21 Negotiating Strategies with Tactics and Defenses

CHAPTER TEN

How to Negotiate with the Opposite Sex

The Road to Building Wealth and Creating Happiness

The Long Way

You have that sinking feeling again. You know—like that gut-wrenching pang the split second after you shut your car door and remember, too late, that the keys are locked inside. This time it's the discontentment after you've suddenly realized that you either paid too much for something, sold too low, or said something that strained a personal or professional relationship. We've all felt this anxiety after failing to get the best deal possible on something we wanted or needed.

You might have come up short in an employment agreement, lost money purchasing or selling a car, or failed at persuading a potential business client to do something. Maybe you're dissatisfied with the demands in a divorce settlement or prenuptial contract. Maybe you're apprehensive about the expected responsibilities in a relationship, or frustrated after failing to resolve a conflict with a family member or coworker.

Most of us have agonized over issues like these at one time or another. So why do we cheat ourselves out of obtaining what we really want or need to feel satisfied? The answer lies in our lack of knowledge about **negotiation**. What does negotiation have to do with it? Everything!

We all negotiate more than we realize. Sure, we define negotiations primarily as the deal-making between a salesperson and a customer, between labor and management, between world leaders. But negotiations permeate our everyday lives. Much of our daily communication with other people falls into the category of negotiation. It's therefore crucial that we learn negotiation skills, not only for business but for our personal lives as well.

Why do we often fail to make the best deals possible? Many people don't recognize that everyday situations are negotiations. Others find negotiating stressful, or their lack of patience steers them to the bottom line too quickly. Some people are inflexible in their thinking and build barriers to agreements. And many people mistake tricks and manipulative behavior for effective negotiating.

Since we all negotiate throughout our lives, we all develop our own negotiating styles. We make deals using strategies and techniques that we've picked up over the years. But the critical questions remain: Do you possess effective negotiation skills, or are you using a disorganized collection of manipulative tactics? Are you negotiating with a life strategy for building wealth and creating happiness, or are you shooting from the hip on almost every deal?

INSTANT NEGOTIATOR addresses these questions—and more. It unlocks the secrets to building a more fulfilling life through the power of skillful negotiating. The INSTANT NEGOTIATOR system is a negotiation strategy based on empathy, skillful communication, imaginative thinking, strong ethics and morals, and a sincere desire to satisfy all people involved in the negotiation. Most importantly, the system helps you recognize and enhance the talents you already possess, and leverage them to create wealth and personal fulfillment. And it offers you a road map that directs you away from common negotiation mistakes that make life a difficult journey.

The Hard Way

He staggered into his wife's hospital room smelling of alcohol, too drunk to notice the lipstick stain on his shirt collar. But his eighteen-year-old wife couldn't have left the lipstick there. She had been in labor that night in August 1955, giving birth to their son. His shameful act of betrayal on the birthday of their child set the stage for the couple's divorce two years later.

That's how my life started. I was that baby boy. Needless to say, my life didn't get off to a great start. My mother, a child herself, struggled with her new role as a nurturer. My father preferred the companionship of a whiskey bottle over that of a wife and son.

What I lost as a child, in terms of a fulfilling family life, I gained in learning about hard work and developing negotiation skills. Could my unhappy family life back then have motivated me to use work as an escape? Maybe. But I'm more inclined to believe that I followed my passion, knowing that nothing could stop me from achieving the life I wanted.

I spent my childhood making friends with, and learning negotiation skills from, neighborhood businessmen like our landlord, Mr. Lindsey. He would take me along when he collected rents door-to-door in our apartment building. I watched and listened as he negotiated with tenants. He also put me to work raking leaves, picking up trash, and doing other maintenance jobs around the apartment house. The work made me productive, and all the while I was learning negotiation skills.

With the money I earned from Mr. Lindsey, I began purchasing old, broken-down bicycles. I would fix them, clean them up, and sell them at a profit to other kids in the neighborhood. Right after high school, I purchased a used tow truck and ran my own towing business. Towing cars put me in contact with a lot of people who wanted to sell their junk cars. I would buy the junkers, fix them up, and sell them at a profit. Two years later, at the age of nineteen, I took my profits from the towing company and launched a real estate career.

My first big real estate negotiation involved buying a dilapidated hotel in Asbury Park, New Jersey. Once again, I was in the business of buying something old, fixing it up, and selling it. The deal paid off. I sold the hotel and made a respectable profit of more than $200,000.

Those were the early days of my twenty-five years in the business world. By 1998, at the age of forty-three, I had negotiated hundreds of successful business transactions and an untold number of satisfying personal agreements as well. I had built Frank D'Alessandro Commercial Realtors, Inc., into the most dominant commercial real estate firm in Fort Myers, FL. I then merged my company with an affiliate of commercial real estate giant

Grubb & Ellis, a multinational corporation publicly traded on the New York Stock Exchange. As CEO, I led Grubb & Ellis - VIP/D'Alessandro as it became the largest and most profitable company of its kind along Florida's southwest coast. In 1999, I sold my share of the company and founded the American Negotiation Institute.

This last achievement was the culmination of my years of developing, refining, and using the INSTANT NEGOTIATOR system in all of my daily negotiations. I used it to personally negotiate multimillion-dollar deals with national retail companies, major banks, and multinational corporations. Looking back at the majority of my negotiations, I recognize that my system not only helped me make profitable deals, it also helped me build valuable business and personal relationships.

Why do I think it's important to tell you about my life? Because I want to make a point about what it takes to gain financial independence and create personal fulfillment. Reflecting on my life, I asked myself the question, "What was it that helped me create the success I had always hoped for?" I thought about this question for weeks, maybe months. Time and again the only answer that came to mind was "my negotiation skills."

It wasn't just that I was conducting business in buying and selling things. I was applying effective negotiation skills in every transaction. Those skills helped me buy the bikes, cars, real estate, and other investments at the lowest prices possible, and to negotiate effectively in selling them at the highest prices possible. The negotiation skills made the difference.

Many people call negotiation an art. Some may imply that the "art" of negotiating means that you must be born with a natural talent to be a good negotiator. I disagree. My experience has taught me that we're not born with negotiation skills: we learn them. I learned mine at a very young age and developed a passion for negotiating. Over the years I developed and refined the INSTANT NEGOTIATOR system that I'm even more passionate about. With this book, I hope to impart to you some of that passion, along with my powerful negotiation system.

Even if you consider yourself an expert negotiator, you'll find value in INSTANT NEGOTIATOR because of its unique, systematic approach. Many people find success in their negotiations. But few use a complete, systematic approach that brings success on a consistent basis. That's the secret to the INSTANT NEGOTIATOR system. When you follow it, step by step, it creates a winning strategy for making fair agreements consistently, while protecting you from people who are trying to win at your expense.

The INSTANT NEGOTIATOR Way

The INSTANT NEGOTIATOR system is an easy-to-learn, principle-based, five-step system for negotiating all types of deals. It's a unique approach that takes into consideration the typical behaviors of people. It helps you understand the psychology of how and why people act the way they do in the negotiation process, and how you can adapt your negotiating style to deal with different types of negotiators.

The skills you learn from this book will give you the confidence and power to negotiate like a professional. You'll learn how to recognize a negotiable situation. And you'll learn how and when to gracefully walk away if you're being taken for a ride. If you negotiate as part of your job, you'll learn a powerful system that will enhance the negotiation skills you already use.

The INSTANT NEGOTIATOR system helps you recognize the true wants and needs of people, and shows you how to meet their needs without sacrificing your own. You'll learn how to protect yourself from unethical people trying to win at your expense. You'll also learn how to tailor your negotiating style in a manner as unique as the person with whom you are negotiating.

If the mere word "negotiation" ties a knot in your stomach, you're not alone. Many people think of negotiation as a stressful battle of wits or a war of words. But your negotiations don't have to be strong-willed "arm wrestling" contests between two adversaries. INSTANT NEGOTIATOR teaches you how to create cordial negotiations. You'll welcome the chance to apply your new negotiation skills.

Overcoming an aversion to negotiating carries a huge payoff. A successful negotiator can cultivate stronger relationships and build great wealth. Family members can avoid arguments, salespeople can close more deals, and business owners can boost their incomes without increasing their workloads using the negotiation skills offered in this system.

Throughout my life, I not only practiced negotiating regularly, I also became a student, researching hundreds of books and attending numerous seminars on the topic. Nothing I found offered a systematic approach for negotiating both professional and social situations. You'll find that my system simplifies the process in any type of negotiation. It turns your daily negotiations into life-enhancing experiences.

Whether you're a corporate executive, small-business owner, middle manager, salesperson, homemaker, hourly employee, or student, the INSTANT NEGOTIATOR five steps guide you toward negotiating the best deal possible for yourself or anyone else on whose behalf you are negotiating.

When you adopt a strategy of negotiating life's challenges, day by day, the accumulation of these small, successful negotiations compounds over time and leads you toward your goals. INSTANT NEGOTIATOR furnishes you with a life strategy that changes the way you see your business and personal life. It helps you recognize the power you have to get what you want and need.

If you know how to drive a car, you already hold an advantage in learning the INSTANT NEGOTIATOR system. Throughout the book, I illustrate many points with the Guiding Traffic Sign Memory System™, which comprises six common traffic signs. These signs help you navigate your way through the negotiation principles and concepts.

I also use stories to make valuable points. Some of the stories come from my first-hand experience. Others I've read or heard throughout my career. In the stories that I know are true, the names of some of the people and places have been changed. This was necessary to protect confidentiality. Truth or fiction, the stories provide definitive examples of negotiating points, and they help convey those points as clearly as possible.

You're on Your Way

To get the most out of this book, you'll need to temporarily set aside your negotiating style. Read INSTANT NEGOTIATOR with an open mind. Learn the system first. Then compare it with your old style. You'll see how INSTANT NEGOTIATOR can give you the confidence to negotiate like a professional and create a better life for you and your family.

The name INSTANT NEGOTIATOR does not imply that your negotiations should happen in an instant. On the contrary, successful negotiators exercise extreme patience, and they find an advantage in not being hurried. The word "instant" means that the negotiation skills I teach in this book are transferable, so that you can learn and apply them instantly.

You'll see the results as soon as you put the system into action. But keep in mind that you must practice your skills continually in order to perfect them. The more you practice and use the skills, the better you'll get at negotiating.

INSTANT NEGOTIATOR is not a scheme of tricks or word games. It's not a gimmick or an attempt to manipulate other people. It's an honest, heartfelt, principle-based system of negotiating agreements and solutions to problems. So sit back, relax, and enjoy your ride as you tour the INSTANT NEGOTIATOR road to building wealth and creating happiness!

CHAPTER ONE

Negotiation:
One of Life's Most
Valuable Skills

A Historical Way of Life

Imagine this scenario: You're standing outside with your family, watching fire rip through your home. No lives are in danger, but flames are threatening all the things that money can't replace: the priceless family portrait, your child's first finger painting on the refrigerator, the wedding china, financial papers, and photographs of family vacations. You feel powerless.

Suddenly firefighters arrive. Maybe they can save your cherished mementos? But the firefighters don't attack the blaze as you thought they would. Instead, the fire chief quickly assesses the task ahead for his crew and then begins negotiating with you on his fee.

Firefighters negotiating a fee? It seems like a horrific suggestion. But negotiating the cost of fire fighting was a real practice in ancient Rome. During the Roman Empire, before governments established fire departments, a Roman entrepreneur named Marcus Crassus is said to have negotiated his fee with homeowners before he would save their homes from burning down. Crassus' wealth enabled him to purchase newly developed fire-fighting equipment that the average Roman couldn't afford.

A majority of the homeowners felt their hands were tied. They didn't know how to negotiate effectively with Crassus. Dealing from such a strong position, Crassus ultimately ended up owning most of the homes he saved, becoming Rome's wealthiest landlord.

Fortunately, you'll probably never have to negotiate with firefighters. But the Crassus scenario makes you think about the importance of negotiation. It represents the seemingly insurmountable struggles we often face and the daily challenges we must overcome in our search for a better life. If we're unable to negotiate effectively, we may have a difficult time achieving the wealth and happiness we deserve.

One of Life's Most Valuable Skills

You're probably eager to start learning the INSTANT NEGOTIATOR system and begin creating wealth and happiness. Before you begin, however, you must first understand the nature of the negotiation process and some important concepts that go along with effective negotiating. We'll move through this information quickly and get you right to the system.

What we achieve in life is in direct proportion to how well we negotiate. Let me say that again: *What we achieve in life is in direct proportion to how well we negotiate.* This phrase is worth saying over and over. It underscores the indispensable role negotiation plays in our daily lives. In essence, negotiations are like pieces of a puzzle that, when connected, form a picture that defines your life.

Too many people shoot from the hip and take on each negotiation as if the results won't affect other parts of their lives. To their detriment, these negotiators view each deal as a separate event, with its own circumstances. Occasional success allows these people to claim victory, while failure often brings excuses.

In reality, our daily negotiations weave complicated webs of relationships, both professional and personal, that we must maintain for future negotiations. We regularly negotiate with the same people again and again. We often engage in similar negotiations repeatedly throughout our lives. Therefore, it makes sense for each of us to build a negotiation framework in our lives—a life strategy for making deals.

From a life strategy, we each can draw powerful deal-making skills for all our negotiations, day in and day out. That's the idea behind the INSTANT NEGOTIATOR systematic approach to negotiating. It helps you recognize negotiation as a required skill for living—as necessary as reading and writing.

I'm not suggesting that you should negotiate the same way all the time. On the contrary, each negotiation brings unique challenges and requires flexible thinking. Besides, consistency could weaken your negotiations by making you predictable. The life strategy I'm talking about is a negotiation system that facilitates good communication, imaginative thinking, and control over the process.

Forget the myth that some people are born negotiators with an inherent knack for deal-making. Some people may possess more natural talent, but personality traits or intelligence do not necessarily dictate success or failure. We all have the opportunity to become better negotiators.

Human Nature

Human nature commits us to the negotiation process. We all have different opinions, different interests, different goals, different likes and dislikes. The only way we can all survive with one another is by resolving our opposing interests via negotiation. But we don't always get there. War is a good example of our failure to overcome our opposing interests.

Opposing interests are inevitable in our daily lives. You want to pay X dollars; the salesperson wants you to pay Y dollars. Your boss wants you to handle X responsibilities; you want the Y responsibilities.

In addition to opposing interests, human nature gives us another reason to negotiate: we're all alike. We *share* mutual interests, too. We all want or need food, clothing, shelter, money, safety—the list goes on and on.

Our mutual interests require us to make deals with one another. We begin negotiating early on. Children learn how to use affection as a bargaining chip. Big, loving hugs from children can persuade parents to give in to their demands. Teenagers make deals over who sits in the front seat of the car or how late they're allowed to stay out.

Adults negotiate more consciously. We negotiate salaries with employers and employees. We make deals with business clients. We haggle over terms in an apartment lease, in buying or selling a home or car. People also make deals in estate settlements and over disputes with family members and coworkers.

As our lives become more complex, our deal-making becomes more frequent and more consequential. We negotiate daily responsibilities in our relationships: who will mow the lawn, who will pick up the children from school, who will take out the garbage? On the professional level, purchasers regularly make deals with suppliers, partners settle business differences, lawyers negotiate for their clients, salespeople negotiate with customers, and managers resolve conflicts with subordinates.

All the goods and services you need in your lifetime are controlled or owned by other people. How you negotiate with people determines the direction of your financial and emotional future. Think about the significance of that!

You can only get what you want if you can convince other people to give it to you or to accept something from you on your terms. If you consistently negotiate poorly over items you purchase, you may find that you have a difficult time saving money. If you consistently resolve conflict by giving in to the other party, sacrificing your wants and needs, you may find that you're dissatisfied in your personal life.

If we lack negotiation skills, our interpersonal relationships can suffer serious consequences. Think about the last argument you had with a family member or friend. Was your goal to win, or to make the other person feel better? People naturally want to win their arguments, so they take an adversarial tone. They resort to hurtful tactics like insulting a person's character. Do we really think we can change other people's minds by yelling at them and insulting them? That's definitely not an effective way to reach agreement.

By consistently negotiating effectively, day after day, you earn positive results in the same way that exercising builds a stronger, healthier body over time. Each successful negotiation brings you one step closer to building financial and emotional health.

Communication

Farmer Joe's insurance company refused to pay him the settlement he requested. The company didn't believe Joe's claim that he had suffered permanent injuries. So both sides ended up in court. Joe showed up in front of the judge with casts on his legs and crutches to help him walk.

"Joe, how are you feeling since the accident?" asked the judge.

Joe replied, "Dang terrible, Judge. I reckon I'm hurt so bad I can't ever walk again."

"That's odd," said the judge. "The police report says that after the accident, officers questioned you and you said you were fine."

"Your Honor," Joe replied, "that there information ain't right! You see, I was drivin' my pickup slow down the road 'cause I don't see so good at night. All of a sudden this big eighteen-wheeler came barrelin' out of nowhere and ran me off the road and into a barn full of horses. I hit so hard I flew out of the truck and darn near crushed my skull on the ground. It knocked me out for a few minutes. And when I woke up I saw the deputy standin' over a couple horses. He said they had broke their legs. So he pulled out his rifle and shot 'em. Then he came and stood over me with his gun still smokin'. He looked down at me and asked me how I felt. *That's* when I said I felt fine!"

When I first heard that story I realized that it makes a good point about the potential problems miscommunication causes in our negotiations. Farmer Joe listened to the deputy and heard what he had asked, but Farmer Joe didn't understand the meaning of the deputy's question. As a result, his negotiation for a settlement became difficult.

When people communicate poorly, their negotiations can become a struggle. Problems they're negotiating over can worsen. Negotiation is a form of reciprocal communication that gives us the opportunity to get what we want or need from others. The level of skill at which we communicate partly determines the effectiveness of our negotiations.

Throughout INSTANT NEGOTIATOR, you're going to hear a lot about communication. In subsequent sections of this book we review examples detailing what we mean by "skillful communication" and how it affects each step of the negotiation process. But for now, we're just going to scratch the surface. As you learn the INSTANT NEGOTIATOR system, you'll discover ideas that will help you develop your communication skills.

Skillful communicating means actively listening so you can have a deep understanding of other people. Active listening requires that you ask probing questions as you seek clues that help define a person. For example, you could listen for comments that may reveal a person's emotions, ego, or sophistication level.

Part of the active listening process is clarifying a person's comments by repeating them. Begin with phrases such as: **"So you think..."** or **"Let me see if I understand your comment; you said..."** The whole idea is to spend more time listening than talking so you can deeply understand other people.

As a skillful communicator, you'll want to keep an open mind about people with different cultural backgrounds, gender, and use of language (such as slang, jargon, and colloquialisms). Also crucial is the ability to adapt your style of speaking to the different people with whom you negotiate. This doesn't mean that you should put on an act to accommodate different people. There's no substitute for being genuine. But since you'll be negotiating with all types of people from all walks of life, you'll want to speak appropriately for each situation so that each person clearly understands what you're presenting.

Management is a form of negotiation that relies heavily on skillful communication. Managers face the monumental task of balancing each team member's personal needs with the company's desire for profits. Many times the two conflict. Workers may need time off to handle legitimate personal issues while the company might already be short-handed. An employee might demand a raise when the company is trying to reduce overhead. Successful managers rely on good communication to negotiate on this thin line between meeting the needs of employees and orchestrating a staff's productivity to the desires of the company.

When negotiators fail in their communication, the deal-making can become inefficient. The process can evolve into a time-consuming and challenging battle of wills. In some cases the negotiations can end tragically, as with the Vietnam War.

Former Secretary of Defense Robert McNamara, in his book *Argument Without End*, reveals a frustrating truth about Vietnam. He explains how it might have been stopped some six years earlier, had the American and North Vietnamese policy makers understood one another more clearly in their efforts to communicate their positions.

McNamara explains how he and other officials working under President Lyndon Johnson misunderstood the mind-set of the Hanoi government, and how Hanoi leaders misinterpreted Washington's request for negotiations. McNamara says that Johnson administration officials believed at the time that the North Vietnamese leaders had no interest in negotiating a settlement to the war. But they were wrong. McNamara concludes that he and other U.S. officials failed to communicate effectively with the Hanoi government. They didn't understand the Hanoi government's point of view. They failed to recognize the other side's real interests.

How crucial is good communication? Ask anyone who lost a family member or friend in Vietnam.

An Alternative to Hostility

Television talk shows have come a long way since Merv Griffin and Mike Douglas. Their shows in the 1970s featured popular movie actors talking about their latest films, or the latest rock-and-roll star playing a hit tune. But now, television is cluttered with talk shows that feature aggressive, even violent behavior. People don't talk anymore—they fight. People scream, yell, and punch one another. They throw chairs and even spit at each other.

Hostile behavior, it seems, has become an acceptable method of conflict resolution, especially in American culture. Newspapers around the country report on husbands and wives beating each other, teenagers settling differences with guns, and neighbors from different cultural backgrounds rioting in the streets of major cities.

How did we come to all this hostility? Maybe that's a complex question with many answers, one for sociologists to ponder. Author and researcher Deborah Tannen, in her book *The Argument Culture*, suggests that we have developed an "argument culture" in our country, which is perpetuated in part by the media. Tannen writes, "The argument culture . . . rests on the assumption that opposition is the best way to get anything done."

People tend to negotiate with their hearts, their passions. And sometimes passion overrides intellect. When people frequently choose argument over negotiation with people they know, the accompanying hostility grinds at the building blocks of a relationship and results in resentment. Over time the resentment becomes overwhelming, and the relationship collapses. When this happens, spouses divorce, children alienate their parents, siblings become strangers, friends become enemies, employees become competitors, partners become rivals, and clients become former clients.

Negotiation might not be the cure for all hostility and violence. But people who follow a system of thoughtful, reasonable, courteous, and patient negotiating to resolve conflict will find that they can control their anger and reduce their chances of becoming involved in a heated argument or fistfight.

Controlling anger is easier said than done. How many times have you promised yourself that you would not become angry with someone, and as soon as you began talking about the issue, you lost control again? Sometimes people will hide their anger, but they'll still "negotiate" with the intention of punishing their opponents. These kinds of behaviors are counterproductive to reaching agreement.

A better understanding of why people react with anger or vengeance might help you avoid it. A person's emotional responses arise from built-in convictions. People become angry when those convictions are threatened. Our brains are hard-wired to fight off threats. When we feel physically threatened, anger allows us to vigorously defend ourselves. Here's where the problem comes in. People mistakenly perceive other people's opinions as threats. But they're not always real threats! Our minds create the threats. In fact, many times we overreact. We incorrectly learn over time that we must argue and fight to defend our points of view. But we don't always need to fight.

Take the case of the employee who asked his manager for holiday pay. "I understand that we're not receiving holiday pay for Christmas just because it falls on a Saturday. Why is that?"

The manager responded with anger, "Look—I'm sick and tired of you damn employees asking me this. If you don't like the damn policy, then quit!"

Was the manager really being threatened enough to warrant such defensive behavior? Couldn't he have simply stated the policy and ended the conversation? Of course, but some people do not have the maturity level to control their anger. Many adults who threw temper tantrums as children continue that behavior throughout their lives.

Threatening or offending an opponent is useless. Anger or criticism makes others unreceptive. You can't argue someone into making a good deal. A better solution is thinking through the issue at hand without responding impulsively. (In Chapters Four through Eight, which detail the INSTANT NEGOTIATOR five steps, I'll discuss strategies for dealing with your opponents' anger and other negative emotions.) Use the following strategies to help keep *your* anger from tainting your negotiation strategy.

1. Don't give in to negative behavior. Stop and think about what you're feeling. Assess your emotions honestly. Ask yourself if you've been offended by something a person did or said. Are you feeling fear, frustration, pressure, or any other emotion that coexists with the anger? People often mask their fear and anxiety with other emotions. Anger is an action-oriented emotion. When you act out your anger, it gives you a false sense that you've accomplished something. Realize that behaving according to your anger does not help your negotiation.

2. Keep your eye on the goal. People often act out or express their impulsive thoughts when they're confronted by someone else. They may respond defensively with insults or accusations. Exposing another person's inadequacies prompts the person to bring up *your* flaws. This leads to an endless argument about who is more blameworthy.

Hostile behavior is a reflex action that's usually not well thought out. In your negotiations, work hard at controlling your impulses. You can choose not to become angry. By controlling your behavior you can defuse the anger. Eliminate any thoughts of retaliation against your opponent. Depersonalize the negotiation. Focus on the goal, not on satisfying your urge to get even. You're not always in the negotiation to achieve emotional comfort (as in some personal negotiations). You're there to achieve a goal.

3. Defuse the anger. In some cases, when you become angry, try telling your opponent how you feel without acting angry. This behavior may allow you to vent your emotions while defusing the anger. It may also help you make your point without threatening your opponent or provoking him or her to act defensively. When you present your feelings, simultaneously offer potential solutions so your opponent knows you're seeking a resolution, not just complaining. Use phrases such as: **"Would you consider...?"** or **"How about...?"** These suggest that you're interested in finding a solution—not arguing.

If you and your spouse or significant other argue over money issues, negotiation skills could save your relationship. Mental health professionals suggest that in ninety percent of all divorces, couples have argued over the lack of money or the control over it. Studies show that when money is lacking, people find it easier to blame their partners for either earning too little or spending too much. And when couples argue over control of money, they sometimes fail to share control of other aspects of the marriage as well.

As former Israeli Prime Minister Golda Meir was quoted as saying, "We can't shake hands with clenched fists." Keep that in mind if you're feeling angry!

Knowing What You Want

A woman walking down a city street stopped to look at some used merchandise in a street peddler's pushcart. She spent a minute or two examining an old frying pan with a bent handle.

"How much is it?" she asked.

"A penny," answered the street peddler.

"Oh...I don't know," said the woman, shaking her head doubtfully.

"Go ahead," urged the peddler. "Make me an offer."

The street peddler had a sense of humor. But the woman didn't have a sense of what she really wanted. If she didn't even want to pay a penny, why would she bother to express some interest? Maybe she felt sorry for the peddler. Or maybe she felt obligated to consider buying something since she had stopped to look.

Have you ever begun a negotiation without really knowing what you wanted? This is a common mistake. Some people do this to help themselves make up their own minds about what they want. Others might feel obligated to at least begin the negotiation for some reason. Whatever the reason, you should know what you want from the negotiation before you begin the process. Write your wants down on a piece of paper to help you clarify in your own mind what your real goal is.

A Satisfying Proposition

Marty was the top salesperson at a well-known electronics store. One day Marty approached her boss about a raise. "Mr. Thomas, I've been working in your store for two years now. I have never missed a day of work. And I know more about the electronics we sell than any other salesperson. With that in mind, I would like you to grant me a ten-percent raise."

Mr. Thomas, a seasoned negotiator, had anticipated Marty's request. "Marty," said Mr. Thomas, "you're right! You have never missed a day, and you are extremely knowledgeable. So I'm glad you brought that up. I've been thinking about promoting you to assistant store manager. The position would make you an important person in our company—a leader. Along with having authority over the other staff, you would receive a four-percent pay raise."

Marty, who had never even considered a promotion, jumped at the opportunity. She found satisfaction in a four-percent raise and a new title. Mr. Thomas kept his best employee while controlling his labor costs. At the end of that negotiation, both Marty and Mr. Thomas were satisfied.

Satisfaction! The Rolling Stones rock group wrote a song about it. They realized it's something everyone wants in life. Isn't that the reason we negotiate—to feel satisfied? Let's face it—people negotiate for more than price, terms, or benefits. That's why the same products under negotiation with different people can sell for different prices. People are satisfied when their expectations are met, and each person has his or her own individual expectations.

Too many negotiators fail to recognize the importance of reaching satisfaction for both sides. Many negotiations start off with each side taking a position. Then, as the negotiation progresses, each person gradually backs off the position, making sacrifices and compromises. That's poor negotiating for two reasons. First, when negotiators focus on positions, they have little flexibility, and the end result often leaves at least one person dissatisfied. Secondly, many people become defensive or hostile when they believe their positions are being threatened.

Effective negotiation is all about understanding interests, not positions, and trying to satisfy the interests of the other person without sacrificing your own. If all interests are satisfied, then the parties have negotiated successfully.

The disparity in medical malpractice suits makes the point about the need for satisfaction. Most medical malpractice suits are settled out of court. The people involved feel satisfied by settling. If they didn't, more cases would go to trial. Even so, a settlement for the same type of lawsuit could range from fifty thousand dollars to a quarter of a million dollars or more. Why do some people settle for so much less? They expect less and therefore are satisfied with less.

Is it possible to get what you asked for in a negotiation and still not feel satisfied? Absolutely! An art dealer named John experienced this dilemma. John travels throughout his home state of Florida, buying and selling artwork. One weekend, at an estate sale, John found a valuable Monet print and quickly began his negotiation.

"I'm on my way to several art sales and I have no time to waste. I'll give you seventy-five dollars for the print," said John. He knew the print was worth at least five times that amount, but he was starting with a low offer. The owner replied, "Seventy-five dollars? OK, it's yours."

John quickly paid the money and left. But moments later he started to feel uncomfortable about his new purchase. He couldn't understand why the owner had accepted his low offer so quickly. Was there something wrong with the print? Did he err in his belief that the print was authentic? John got a great deal—but no satisfaction.

In essence, the seller's quick acceptance of the offer left John dissatisfied. What could John have done ahead of time to ensure satisfaction? He could have inquired more about the seller's motivation. He would have learned that the house where the estate sale was being held had been sold. The seller was more concerned about selling off all the furnishings immediately than he was about getting the best prices.

This story also presents a lesson to the seller. He would have satisfied John had he rejected the first offer. He could have accepted it later if the sale were in jeopardy.

The lesson: Never accept the first offer.

You've probably heard that the three most important issues to consider when buying real estate are location, location, location. In your negotiations it's satisfaction, satisfaction, and satisfaction.

In fact, satisfaction is the most important goal in any negotiation. Without satisfaction, an agreement is not likely.

The Danger of Compromise

How would you like it if you lived your life with only a fifty-fifty chance of obtaining what you wanted or needed to be happy? That's what compromise offers. It's a common method that people use for solving problems or reaching agreements. And some people tout compromise as an amicable way of reaching agreements. The problem is that it doesn't bring satisfaction to either side. Instead, it requires people to sacrifice their own interests and settle for less.

Writer Leo Stein reportedly said this about compromise: "A temporary compromise is a diplomatic act, but a permanent compromise is an abandonment of a goal."

Because compromise is the path of least resistance, it rarely achieves the best result for either side. So the next time someone says to you, "Let's split the difference," stop and think about whether the compromise really gets you what you want. President Woodrow Wilson was quoted as saying, "Better to go down fighting than to dip your colors in dishonorable compromise."

In Chapter Six, "Step 3: Introduce New Alternatives," I'll show you a better way than compromising.

Summary

- ⏱ "What we achieve in life is in direct proportion to how well we negotiate."

- ⏱ By simply being human, you are already a negotiator.

- ⏱ Effective negotiation is a transferable skill that anyone can learn.

- ⏱ Effective negotiating adds value to your life.

- ⏱ The consequences of poor negotiating can cause financial and emotional hardship.

- ⏱ Negotiation is an important alternative to hostile arguments.

- ⏱ Know what you want before you begin negotiating.

- ⏱ A successful negotiator always strives for satisfaction.

- ⏱ Compromise requires people to make unwanted sacrifices and settle for less.

CHAPTER TWO

The Nature of Negotiation: Mind-sets and Fundamentals

Conflicting Mind-sets

INSTANT NEGOTIATOR points out a lot of negative behaviors in poor negotiators. You'll learn how to recognize ineffective negotiating practices ahead of time and keep yourself from making common mistakes. Poor negotiators usually possess a "conflicting mind-set." Conflicting mind-sets run counter to the basic principles of negotiating fair deals. They drive people to make decisions based on the dynamics of their personalities, not on the facts of their negotiations. In other words, people often negotiate from how they feel emotionally instead of from thinking pragmatically.

Learning the conflicting mind-sets can help you avoid making mistakes and help you identify problems that your opponents present in the deal. The four conflicting mind-sets are: Acceptors, Fearfuls, Selfers, and Controllers.

The "Acceptor"

A budding car collector named Don answered a classified ad that read: *For Sale: Mint Condition '59 Caddy.* Don had been searching for a vintage

Cadillac. He wasted no time. He met briefly with the owner and examined the car. Then he moved enthusiastically to the bottom line.

"How much do you want?" asked Don.

The owner replied, "I'm asking eighteen thousand dollars."

Don was shocked. He knew that a 1959 Cadillac in mint condition should have carried a value of at least twenty thousand dollars at the time. Don quickly wrote a check for the asking price and drove off in his vintage Cadillac.

Don was positive that he had gotten a good deal. But did he get the best deal possible? Don never "tested" the price quoted by the seller—meaning he never bothered to offer less than the asking price. Don later learned that the seller had inherited the car. He had no interest in vintage cars and was frustrated that the car was taking up space in his garage. The seller would have accepted less than the asking price just to get rid of it. But Don had never even considered negotiating for a better price.

Don possessed the type of negotiation mind-set I call the "Acceptor." These negotiators commonly miss out on chances to negotiate the best deal for themselves because they simply accept the first offer. They don't typically question the price, terms, or benefits of things they negotiate. They accept an opponent's opinion as fact. And, many times, Acceptors don't recognize when they're in the midst of a negotiation or when the opportunity for a better deal exists.

The gentle nature of Acceptors can make them weak negotiators. They are usually peaceful, diplomatic people. But they are often even-tempered and tolerant of others to a fault. Because Acceptors often go out of their way to accommodate other people, they worry about insulting their opponents. They're reluctant to request too much from them. Acceptors often become submissive under pressure. They seek acceptance by making unnecessary concessions and compromises, hoping to avoid confrontation. Acceptors also feel more comfortable giving than taking, and they often feel undeserving of a better deal.

If you possess any of the Acceptor's tendencies, you can improve your negotiating skills by starting with "testing" the price. That means you should almost always assume the price written down or quoted to you can be adjusted. You can't get the best deal possible unless you ask for it.

Let's be realistic though—not everything is negotiable. It makes little sense to make low offers on a loaf of bread or a gallon of milk. But when you put yourself in a mind-set that most things are negotiable, you will also begin to recognize more opportunities to use your negotiation skills.

The "Fearful"

President John F. Kennedy once said, "Let us never negotiate out of fear, but let us never fear to negotiate." Kennedy made a good point. Many people shy away from negotiating because they fear the process. I call people with this mind-set "Fearfuls." They mostly fear being rejected if they ask for a better deal. Fearfuls often worry about losing out on whatever they're negotiating over, or they're afraid of appearing ignorant in the eyes of other people.

Fearfuls usually possess endearing traits. They're honest, loyal, and empathetic. But they are also dangerously emotional and insecure. Fearfuls are "worrywarts," and they often feel intimidated by the negotiation process, uncertain of where to start or what to say. They usually have good intentions, desiring a fair agreement. But the negotiation process becomes emotionally agonizing because they feel so awkward.

Rather than making tough, logical decisions, Fearfuls often react to their emotions in hopes of minimizing their anxiety. Consequently, they make quick concessions and compromises just to end the pain of the negotiation.

How do you overcome the fear of negotiating? One solution is to "desensitize" yourself. Make a habit of asking for a better deal in every negotiable situation. The repetition will eventually dissolve the fear. Negotiating actually becomes enjoyable as time goes on and as you hone your skills.

Many Fearfuls need a step-by-step plan to guide them through the negotiation process. Having a plan helps them eliminate the fear of appearing unprepared and satisfies their desire for perfection. The INSTANT NEGOTIATOR five-step system is the best plan to move the Fearful through the negotiation process.

The "Selfer"

Jim is threatening to sue his employer, Karen, over a company policy issue. Jim claims that the employer unfairly withheld part of his paycheck to pay for a laptop computer that Jim damaged when he took it home to complete office work.

Company policy says that any employee who takes company equipment out of the office and damages it must pay for the replacement. While Jim contends that the computer was old and simply broke down, the employer contends that Jim must have dropped it.

"I want my money back, or I'm taking you guys to court," Jim calmly threatens.

"Look, Jim," Karen responds, "I don't want this to turn into a power struggle. It's clear you understood the policy before you took the computer home. But since we disagree on how the computer was damaged, let's find a fair solution so we both can get back to work."

"The only fair solution is to give me the rest of my paycheck," Jim counters.

"But our engineering department proved that you damaged the unit, so you're liable," says Karen. "But in order to settle this quickly, I'm willing to find a fair solution for you and the company."

"Forget it," says Jim. "The company can afford to buy a new computer. I can't on my salary."

"Are you telling me you won't even consider paying part of the cost?" asks Karen.

"I'm telling you that I will sue this company if I don't get all my pay," says Jim.

"Well, have your lawyer contact our legal department," says Karen. "I'll see you around."

Unfortunately for Jim, he's the type of person who negotiates with the mind-set that only two options exist—winning or losing. These negotiators are called "Selfers." They rarely consider the other side's wants and needs.

Jim knew that he was liable for the computer; he was simply fighting to win the negotiation, rather than finding a fair solution.

Selfers are usually self-possessed negotiators. They don't always have bad intentions. In fact, most of the time they are enthusiastic and fun loving. But their selfishness limits the options available to each side. They base much of their preparation for the negotiation on their own positions, without considering the other side's interests. If the negotiation does not go exactly as they planned, Selfers tend to blame others, preferring to save face rather than collaborate on a better solution.

When Selfers lack the power to get what they want, they sometimes will take whatever is offered because they fail to recognize alternatives. At other times, these negotiators harbor a self-absorbed, win-at-all-costs mentality. They typically don't consider that both sides can—and should—win in a negotiation. Selfers may also be irresponsible and can fail to live up to agreements. They're usually charismatic, and friendly, but their poor listening skills leave little opportunity for reaching agreements that satisfy everyone in the deal.

How do you overcome a Selfer's mind-set? Think big-picture. Seek alternatives that will benefit both sides. A person who feels as if he or she has lost in a negotiation could fail to live up to an agreement. By considering the other side's interests, you don't have to worry about policing an opponent to make sure he or she follows through. In Jim's case, he could have listened to Karen's alternatives, offered his own alternatives, then worked out an agreement that would have solved the problem quickly and fairly.

The "Controller"

"Listen, pal!" Hank argued. "You send me the insurance papers today or I'm recommending that my client use another company."

"But, Hank, we can't complete the insurance policy because your client didn't bring in the check we requested a week ago," Ken explained.

"I don't want your lame excuses. You don't need that check to get me what I need. I've been an attorney for ten years, and I've never dealt with such an incompetent company as yours. Now get me those papers today," Hank demanded.

That's an example of the Controller's mind-set in negotiations. Controllers try to manipulate people, sometimes with anger. They either do this intentionally or, like Selfers, they mistake negotiation for a contest of wills. Controllers may also react emotionally instead of thinking objectively. Their impatience makes them bottom-line-oriented. They become dictatorial under pressure and defensive at the slightest hint that they should concede something. Sometimes Controllers are insensitive, and they tend to exude a strong self-confidence. Sometimes they are intolerant and judgmental of people who don't live up to their standards.

The Controller's assertive and often selfish style sometimes results from a deep personal insecurity. Many Controllers seek the acceptance that they usually refuse to give others.

Controllers think in terms of win/lose, taking little time to listen to opponents or to brainstorm solutions with them. They demand control, and they find power in being authoritative. They're more likely to walk away from a deal if they become offended or as a matter of "principle" if they think they're losing control.

Controllers waste a lot of energy trying to control other people. It's unnecessary to control people, especially if you have control of the negotiation process. Avoid the Controller's mind-set by giving your opponents the incentive to consider your interests, namely by taking into account *their* interests and conceiving alternatives that add value to the deal for them.

Do You Have a Conflicting Mind-set?

You need to understand mind-sets ahead of time for two reasons:

1. You want to identify whether you have one of the conflicting mind-sets. Be honest with yourself. Is one predominant, or are several present when you negotiate?

2. You need to identify your opponent's mind-set. If an opponent possesses an Acceptor, Fearful, Selfer, or Controller mind-set, then you can counter with a more effective negotiating style offered by the INSTANT NEGOTIATOR five-step system.

The INSTANT NEGOTIATOR system will help you eliminate your conflicting mind-set if you have one, and it'll defend you against others who possess them. The system focuses on building amicable relationships among negotiating parties. It requires you to empathize with people and understand their interests. It offers strategies on how to keep your emotions under control while finding creative ways to deal with the other person's concerns. The system seeks alternatives that add value so that each side can walk away from the negotiation satisfied.

Fundamentals in Every Negotiation

Every negotiation embodies three fundamentals that could play a role in your negotiation strategy. They are **time**, **power**, and **knowledge**. These fundamentals can either give you control of the negotiation process or take control away from you.

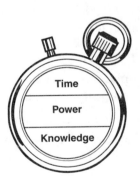

Time

All negotiations have a time limit. The time limit is set by the wants and needs of the people involved. Once you've determined how much time you have, you'll then determine the pace at which you move through the INSTANT NEGOTIATOR five-step system. For example, if you're negotiating the cost of a gym membership, the time you have to complete the negotiation may range from only minutes to hours. When resolving a conflict between yourself and your employer, the negotiation may take days or weeks. If you're an international negotiator seeking peace in the Middle East, you may be negotiating for years.

Time can be used as a tool in the deal-making process. When you have more time than your opponent, you have an advantage, especially when you know your opponent's deadline. My research taught me about time tactics used by Japanese businessmen. When an American counterpart would visit Japan to hammer out a deal, the Japanese businessmen would learn about the American's hotel reservations and his scheduled time to return home. They would drag out the negotiations until the final hours before the American would have to get to the airport, forcing the American to negotiate an agreement hastily and to the benefit of the Japanese businessmen.

When the Japanese negotiators visited the U.S., they purchased one-way tickets, and rented apartments month-to-month basis, implying that they had months to spend on the negotiation. This tactic kept the Americans from dragging out the negotiation until the last minute, because the Japanese appeared to be under no time pressure.

Power

In negotiation, power often emanates from people's perceptions. Have you ever been intimidated during a job interview when you had to answer questions from the president of the company? The title "president" gives the perception that power exists. Many times the only power people have in a negotiation is the power that an opponent allows because of his or her perceptions. Your perception of yourself could either give you power or take it away.

Real power can exist too. Indifference is an example of one form of real power. If you have no emotional attachment to a deal, you can refuse to make concessions and walk away easily.

Information is also power. The more information you have about the issue and your opponent, the more you can negotiate alternatives that will satisfy everyone in the negotiation.

You'll have opportunities to equalize the power between yourself and your opponents. Many times, by increasing your power, you consequently diminish your opponent's power. One way you can give yourself negotiating power is by exhibiting confidence. Your opponents may recognize your confidence. They may perceive you as an authoritative figure or an expert. Those perceptions generate your negotiating power.

People often enter their negotiations believing that the other person has more power over them. But many times that power is overestimated. Always remember to go into your negotiations with confidence. Building confidence and demonstrating it plays a major role in negotiating successfully. The INSTANT NEGOTIATOR five steps further cover confidence building.

Knowledge

If you were negotiating the price of a diamond, you would want to understand the differences in the color, clarity, cut, and carats of diamonds and how they influence value. Your knowledge of those elements provides an edge in negotiating a favorable price.

Whether you're negotiating responsibilities in a relationship or the terms of a multimillion-dollar contract, having substantial knowledge of the issue gives you negotiating power. Knowledge of your opponent's goals in the negotiation also strengthens your ability to negotiate successfully. The more you know about your opponent's needs, the more accurately you can develop alternatives that he or she will find valuable.

The Guiding Traffic Sign Memory System™

Like following road signs when driving your car, you can follow *The Guiding Traffic Sign Memory System™* when negotiating. The signs are a learning tool. They help you understand and remember important points about the negotiation process. You're going to see them a lot throughout the book. So take the time now to review the signs.

The "Caution" sign is used most often in the book. It signals those times when you must pay close attention to what possibly could go wrong and hurt your negotiation.

Unfortunately many negotiators rush toward an agreement. The "Slow Zone" reminds you that hasty negotiating results in bad deals. The sign encourages patience, and it points out times when you should move slowly through the process.

Negotiations can break down when people don't listen to or understand the other side's point of view. The "Yield" sign identifies times in the negotiation process when you should yield to your opponent by listening more or considering more thoroughly his or her interests. This can help you avoid mis-communication.

Sometimes people see an advantage in redirecting their negotiation strategies. The "Detour" sign offers you a different approach. It points out when a change in your negotiation strategy is necessary.

During your negotiations, you will inevitably run into problems that could block any potential for an agreement. The "Bump" sign identifies typical trouble spots that you can usually overcome. The sign reminds you that many problems are only minor bumps, not deal killers. And we provide advice that guides you over the bumps with little trouble.

One of the most powerful negotiating tools you have is your ability to walk away from a negotiation. Sometimes it's the best alternative. The "Stop" sign tags those times when stopping the negotiation, either temporarily or permanently, will serve your best interests.

Summary

⏱ **"Conflicting mind-sets" (Acceptors, Fearfuls, Selfers, and Controllers) can lead you to failure in your negotiations.**

⏱ **You can learn to eliminate your fear of negotiating.**

⏱ **You can gain confidence and certainty in the negotiation process, and you can negotiate the best deal possible for yourself without engaging in stubborn behavior or inflexible thinking.**

⏱ **The fundamentals in every negotiation are:**
   Time, Power, and Knowledge.

⏱ **The Guiding Traffic Sign Memory System™**
   Caution, Slow Zone, Yield, Detour, Bump, Stop

CHAPTER THREE

The INSTANT NEGOTIATOR Style

Negotiating Styles: A Tender or Tough Approach

An old proverb suggests: "If the mountain won't bend, then you bend the road, and if the road won't bend, then you bend yourself." The INSTANT NEGOTIATOR system follows this line of thinking. It requires flexible thinking on the part of negotiators, especially in their negotiating styles. The system recognizes two extreme negotiating styles: **tender** and **tough**.

These extreme styles are the least effective if you use either one exclusively. The INSTANT NEGOTIATOR system is based on a fluid approach, ranging between tender and tough—a flexible style of negotiating.

Although the system recommends starting with the *tender* approach, it offers *tough* strategies to get what you want from people who try winning at your expense.

The "Conflicting Mind-sets" you learned about earlier (Acceptors, Fearfuls, Selfers, and Controllers) direct negotiators toward the two extreme negotiating styles.

An example of a "tender" negotiating style is exemplified in a quote by actor James Cotton. He reportedly said, "In the end, all we hope to achieve is a high standard of compromise." (Frankly, I don't know what style Mr. Cotton used in his negotiations, but the quote by itself shows a tender style.) People who negotiate with a tender style usually possess either an Acceptor's or Fearful's mind-set. They give in easily to compromises and unnecessary concessions.

At the other end of the spectrum, the "tough" negotiating style usually develops either from the Selfer's or Controller's mind-sets. People who use the tough style may appear inflexible or self-absorbed. The following quote from former Israeli Defense Minister Moshe Dayan implies a tough style: "Once you accept our views, we shall be in full agreement."

While tender negotiators are more likely to *give* concessions, tough negotiators *take* as much as they can get from their opponents. But INSTANT NEGOTIATOR focuses on something other than just *giving* and *taking*. It requires you to add alternatives to the negotiation that the opponents can share in. You examine how, by adding value to the negotiation, both parties have a better chance of achieving their goals. Successful negotiating is much more than merely compromising on what's at stake.

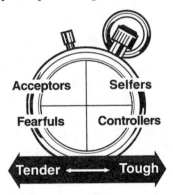

With a flexible style, you can pursue a deep understanding of people, building rapport with your opponents and collaborating—as opposed to competing—when seeking solutions. Flexible thinking allows you to vary your style, accommodating all types of negotiations. You can be persuasive without being overbearing. You can exude confidence without seeming stubborn. You can create a cordial and pleasant negotiating atmosphere. Most of all, a flexible negotiating style helps you think creatively, offering opponents valuable options that make them feel like winners when the negotiation is over.

In our review of the INSTANT NEGOTIATOR five steps, we'll examine further the positives and negatives of the two primary negotiating styles. And we'll discuss how you can adapt your style and add value to achieve the best results.

Patience

You've heard the adage "Patience is a virtue." Well, in negotiation, patience is a requirement if you want to find success.

A number of police hostage negotiation units around the world wear uniform shoulder patches with the words *Semper patientia*. That means "patience always" in Latin. It shows how essential patience is in our negotiations.

Patience is not only crucial to saving a hostage's life. It's paramount to negotiating the best deals possible in everyday situations. Many people have a natural tendency to get right to the bottom line in their negotiations. They move too quickly without knowing ahead of time what consequences they face.

How do you use patience as a strategic edge in your negotiations? First, you have to understand why some negotiators don't exercise patience. Some people feel nervous about negotiating, and they move quickly to end their anxiety. Others may lack self-confidence and try to compensate by being too assertive. And some people simply overlook the value of patience.

Do you have patience in your negotiations, or do you rush to resolve issues as quickly as possible? Think about that question for now. As you move through the INSTANT NEGOTIATOR five steps, pay special attention to "Slow Zone" signs which give tips on how to remain patient while negotiating.

Setting and Changing Expectations

A big part of your negotiating strategy will be setting or changing the expectations of your opponents. For example, when buying a product, you want the seller to expect that you're not willing to pay top dollar.

If your opponent already has an expectation, you want to change it to your benefit. Let's say that same seller thinks he or she can charge you the highest price possible because you have limited time to make the deal.

You can change that expectation by letting the seller know up front that you have an appointment with a competitor who's offering a better price.

Sometimes the best negotiations take place when the participants don't expect to enter a formal negotiation. An opponent once said to me, "I'm ready to negotiate with you." That made me put up my guard and changed my expectation of the meeting from a friendly get-together to a head-to-head competition. If that person simply began by easing into the negotiation process, without essentially saying "let's negotiate," I might have been less cautious and more receptive to his needs.

Expectations and Power

Setting your opponent's expectations to where you want them builds power for you in the negotiation. It gives you control of the negotiation from the start. Many times, it takes power away from your opponent. Does this mean that you want to beat your opponent down by rendering him or her powerless? Absolutely not! It sets the stage for you to build a cordial negotiating environment in which both sides are willing to conceive alternatives that satisfy everyone.

That's where the INSTANT NEGOTIATOR five steps come into play. You use the steps as a systematic approach to controlling the negotiation so the process goes the way you want it to. That's the basis of this negotiating strategy.

Over the next five chapters you're going to learn the INSTANT NEGOTIATOR five-step system. I've dedicated one chapter for each step. From this point on you'll learn how to use the five steps with a style varying from tender to tough, always remaining patient, with the goal of satisfaction in mind.

CHAPTER FOUR

Step 1:
Know Your Opponent

Who Is an Opponent?

In his fight against communism in Poland, Lech Walesa, the man who led the Solidarity movement, is reported to have said, "It is not important with whom I sit down at the table. I'll hold talks with the cleaning lady if she's properly authorized."

Although one might infer that Walesa's comment unjustly demeans the value of a cleaning lady's work, Walesa makes a valuable point about negotiation. He suggests that your "opponent" is anybody with whom you are attempting to reach an agreement. This definition differs somewhat from the popular definition in most dictionaries, which describe "opponent" as an adversary and imply that either side must win or lose. But, for the purposes of negotiation, understand that your opponent is not necessarily an enemy or adversary. And your negotiating strategy should not be based on winning at the expense of your opponent.

Our opponents are people we already know, such as family members, employers, and coworkers. They're people we've just met, such as salespeople and customers. Any person who has an opposing interest or an opposing point of view on a subject of mutual interest, and with whom you are attempting to reach an agreement, is your opponent.

Your opponent is anyone
with whom you are attempting
to reach an agreement.

Knowing your opponent means more than knowing a person's name or face. It's a process of building rapport with people, researching their motivations, and examining what makes them tick and what characterizes them as individuals. Knowing your opponent means, more than anything else, taking a sincere interest in people and empathizing with them before the formal negotiation begins.

You can achieve these goals initially by becoming an expert conversationalist. Dale Carnegie, author of *How to Win Friends and Influence People*, talked a lot about how the best conversationalists are really the best listeners. He makes this point with the story of Mrs. Henrietta Douglas and a department store clerk.

Mrs. Douglas had purchased a new winter coat at a well-known department store, but after returning home she noticed a tear in the lining. When she returned to the store the next day, a clerk refused to even listen to her complaint. Just as Mrs. Douglas was leaving the store, swearing never to shop there again, a manager stopped her and asked about her dilemma. After spending valuable time listening to Mrs. Douglas, the manager offered to repair the coat for free. The manager saved a longtime customer simply by being a good conversationalist—by listening and empathizing with Mrs. Douglas.

Two Human Characteristics

Good conversationalists must be able to identify two basic human characteristics: feelings and beliefs. These characteristics influence our negotiations. Our feelings emerge from our emotional attachment to the issue being negotiated—our love and hate, for example. Beliefs reflect our values, such as the morals, ethics, and principles that we live by. These characteristics live in people's personalities. And it's crucial that you make note of them in your efforts to know your opponents.

Keep the Opponent and the Issue Separate

When negotiators see their opponents not as other people with human characteristics but only as the opposing interest or problem they're faced with, conflict usually arises. That's why it's important to separate the opponent and the issue.

Don't confuse your opponent with the issue.

Residents of a community called Summer Lake experienced this type of conflict because they failed to separate the opponent from the issue. At a controversial neighborhood meeting, homeowners disclosed a plan calling for streetlights in the neighborhood. A resident named Jack had proposed the streetlights. But some neighbors resented Jack's plan. They expressed outrage over his suggestion that each homeowner pay an assessment of two hundred dollars for the cost, plus an increase in the association dues for electricity and maintenance. They argued that if Jack and his supporters wanted streetlights, they should pay the cost themselves.

Finally, after thirty minutes of venting their frustrations, the angry residents yielded the floor to Jack. He calmly explained that he had proposed the streetlights because of something he had read in the newspaper several months earlier. One evening, in a nearby neighborhood, a car had hit and almost killed two children. The driver told police he never saw the children playing in the street because the street was too dark. It had no lighting.

The angry residents of Summer Lake eventually learned that Jack wasn't selfishly fighting for streetlights. He was actually trying to make life safer for them and their children. They also learned a little more about Jack, the person: that he had lived alone in his Summer Lake home for the past two years, ever since his wife and only son had died in a car accident.

Yield to your opponent. Let the person speak so you can clearly understand his or her point of view.

Can you see how the angry residents equated Jack with what they believed were expensive and unreasonable fees? Their feelings and beliefs pitted them against Jack and his supporters, creating conflict at the meeting.

Avoid the "us against them" attitude.

Jack eventually made a deal after several meetings. He and his supporters agreed to phase in streetlights in Summer Lake over an extended period of time at a lower up-front cost. They succeeded in their effort to keep the opponent separate from the issue.

People commonly confuse the opponent with the issue when they negotiate with someone close to them—say a family member, friend, or coworker. The old adage "Familiarity breeds contempt" applies in these cases. We may tend to argue with a familiar opponent without considering precisely why he or she is taking a certain position. This conversation between a teenage boy and his father makes the point:

Son: "Dad, can I borrow the car?"

Father: "Borrow the car again? No! You went joyriding last night.
            You've been putting too many miles on the car lately.
            That's enough for this weekend!"

Son: "C'mon, Dad. I need the car."

Father:	"No, I said!"
Son:	"Why are you so uptight about me driving the car? I only need it for a little while."
Father:	"I don't care how long you need it. I simply don't want you taking the car tonight. That's final!"
Son:	"OK, then. I'll just tell Mom I can't pick up her medicine because I didn't have a way to get to the drugstore."

Don't jump to conclusions.

The son had a good reason to ask his father for the car. But his father looked only at the issue of the car, without trying to understand his son's point of view—his reasons for asking. He jumped to a conclusion.

Avoid Focusing on Positions

The father in the previous example had locked himself into a negotiating position. He held firm on not allowing the son to take the car, even though he was ignorant of his son's and his wife's interests.

People often negotiate to justify their positions, rather than being open-minded about their opponents' interests. The father's position was that he didn't want his son to take his car. But maybe he had other interests, too. He could have been concerned about the son driving in bad weather. Maybe he didn't want to use up gas that he needed for a trip the next day. The father could have had numerous interests that explained his position. But he neither explained his interests nor inquired about his son's. Unfortunately, his negotiation was based solely on a position.

A common business exercise makes the point further. Researchers comparing the differences in the 1980's between American and Japanese business philosophies drew an imaginary line on the floor and placed one person on each side. The purpose was to get one person to convince the other person, without force, to cross the line. American business people almost never convinced one another. But their Japanese counterparts simply said, "If you will cross the line, so will I." They exchanged places, and they both won.

Your negotiations can also fall short when personal relationships become entangled with issues. This happens when one person's poor communication causes the other person to infer that he or she has been accused of creating a problem. John Gray, the well known author of *Mars and Venus Together Forever*, tells the story of how he and his wife Bonnie avoided this predicament.

John wanted to buy a big-screen TV for their living room. Bonnie said she didn't want a big-screen TV "looming" in her living room every day. She was concerned that it would ruin the decor of the room. Gray explains that he became infuriated because he felt forced to give up something he liked just to make his wife happy. But he didn't express his negative feelings. He didn't want to put his wife on the defensive. Instead, Gray calmly explained that he understood his wife's concerns, but that he also had waited a long time to be able to afford a big-screen TV. Gray then asked for his wife's opinion on how they could reach an agreement.

Gray watched his words—and showed respect for his wife's wishes. He also created an environment in which he and his wife could collaborate as a supportive couple in negotiating a solution. Gray neither alienated his wife nor allowed the issue to become entangled in the relationship. After shopping around, Gray and his wife found a television set and living room furniture that they both liked.

Take the time to create a positive environment in which to negotiate.

People in professional relationships, such as business partners and co-workers, can also learn a lesson from Gray's approach. Take the case of the partners in an auto parts store. Tom heads the sales and marketing; Jose runs the operations. Watch how this relationship becomes entangled in the issue.

Jose: "Tom, sales were way down this past quarter. What's the problem with your department?"

Tom: "There's no problem in my department! The market went soft temporarily. There was nothing I could do about it!"

In his negotiation with Tom, Jose alienated his partner. He put Tom on the defensive by relating him to the problem of reduced sales. He also risked damaging their professional relationship. A more effective approach could have avoided the entanglement of the issue and the relationship:

Jose: "Tom, our sales are under budget. Are there any changes we can make in our marketing plan to help sales?"

Notice the difference in Jose's approach? This time he suggests that he and Tom should work together in finding a solution.

Alienation is an enemy of a successful negotiation.

Prejudice Leads Only to Failure

Mary's hands shook as she held the real estate contract. The years had deteriorated Mary's motor skills. But aging didn't stop her from purchasing a new home with all the features she'd ever wanted. Seventy-eight-year-old Mary sat face-to-face with a young, aggressive real estate agent negotiating the deal. By the agent's tone of voice, Mary could sense that he considered her a fragile, little old lady who would be a pushover in the negotiation.

"Just sign your name, dear, and I'll take care of the rest. Don't worry about anything, dear. You're getting a great deal on this home," said the agent.

Mary hated being called "dear." But she kept her cool and began nego-tiating the deal. "I know that similar houses have sold for as much as se-ven thousand dollars less than this asking price. Besides, the houses in this neighborhood are going to be hit with a utility assessment. You see, young man," Mary concluded with a smile, "I know about all these extra costs because I've been a practicing real estate attorney for the last thirty-five years. And I was negotiating deals long before you were born."

What happened here was that the real estate agent fell into a common trap. He had prejudged his opponent. Instead of seeing Mary as a person, he saw her only as a "little old lady" and an easy sale.

Quite often, people draw conclusions about other people based on appear-ance, race, religion, and so on. Some people have biases and simply don't realize it. Conclusions drawn from superficial criteria can provide misin-formation. You cannot truly know a person until you probe more deeply into a person's characteristics. An anonymous quote I read once sums up the point this way:

"Any bias renders the mind incapable of providing accurate information about the actual world."

 It's not only wrong to prejudge people or have biases against them, it's a mistake that usually has costly consequences.

Negotiating with the Right Opponent

In a boxing match you have two "corners" or teams. Each corner includes the fighter, of course, and the trainers who advise him on how to win. I have never seen a fighter run to the opposing corner when the bell rang, and punch one of the trainers. Why not? Because knocking out a trainer doesn't count. The fighter can't succeed that way. The trainer is not the right opponent.

The same holds true for negotiations. You must carefully choose the right opponent. Otherwise, you waste time and you risk failure—especially if you're negotiating by telephone. I've seen people on the telephone give away too much of their negotiating strategies to people who were not authorized to make the final deal.

Unless you already have a personal or professional relationship with your opponent, the concept of recognizing the right opponent may seem unclear to you. The following question can save you a lot of time and wasted effort:

"If I were interested in discussing the final price and terms of this item, are you the person who could make the final decision?"

Be careful, however, about always demanding to meet with top decision-makers when haggling over price and terms. Sometimes salaried managers have less incentive to make concessions. A salesperson will be motivated to negotiate a fair deal if it means closing a sale and earning a commission.

Invest time in learning who the decision-maker is.

Sometimes the right opponent is an outside force such as a spouse or parent who isn't present. A financial planner in Oregon learned this lesson the hard way. He spent two days showing financial investment plans to a nineteen-year-old girl. The girl's parents promised to give her money to invest as a gift for graduating from high school. After negotiating on the financial planner's fee and agreeing on an investment strategy, the girl signed the necessary paperwork and seemed happy with the service. The next day the girl's father charged into the financial planner's office and irately accused him of taking advantage of his daughter. He demanded they cancel the paperwork immediately.

The father, not the daughter, turned out to be the decision-maker because he was the person providing the money. The financial planner made a mistake when he failed to ask the girl if she needed her parents' approval on the service, since they were giving her the money. The financial planner negotiated with the wrong person.

Who's Involved in Our Negotiations

Dean earned a twenty-thousand-dollar bonus at his job as a construction supervisor. So he decided he wanted to buy a boat. But when Dean's wife Victoria learned of her husband's bonus, she immediately envisioned a new swimming pool in their backyard.

At the boat dealership Dean negotiated with a salesman and got a great price on a new boat. But he couldn't sign the papers without telling Victoria about their fabulous deal. What do you think happened when Dean got home and showed Victoria the contract for the boat? Well, Dean's negotiating didn't end at the boat dealership. Victoria obviously entered into the negotiation. And what about Dean's teenage son Billy, who was hoping his father would buy him a car? He became the fourth person in the negotiation.

In the end, Dean ended up with a pool in his backyard and a used car for his son. He may have negotiated effectively with the boat salesman, but his wife and son apparently negotiated from stronger positions. The boat salesman, of course, lost a deal. And he wasted a lot of time negotiating with Dean, not realizing that Victoria and Billy were indirectly involved in the negotiation.

Do you now see how a simple negotiation between two people, a salesman and a buyer, might be ineffective when other people are indirectly involved? Your opponent might have to answer to some other person before he or she is able to reach a final agreement.

The Value of Good Rapport

The famous criminal defense attorney Clarence Darrow once said that even if the facts of a case suggest a defendant's guilt, jury members are less likely to convict if they like the defendant. Many years later, researchers studied Darrow's theory. In hundreds of cases, they found that people who appeared more likable had more positive outcomes in court. This says a lot about how being liked can help in your negotiations.

People prefer to deal with people they like. The easiest way to make people like you is by building rapport. You can build rapport with people you've just met or with people you already know. What separates effective negotiators from others is their conscious decision to slow down and avoid jumping right into a negotiation without building rapport first.

Rapport creates a relationship between opponents. It identifies their compatibility and fosters mutual appreciation. For opponents who already have a relationship, rapport reinforces their affinity for one another, despite the need to negotiate.

Stop yourself from jumping
right into the negotiation.
Build rapport first.

Entrepreneur H. Wayne Huizenga amassed great wealth in large part because of his rapport-building skills. As a young man, Huizenga purchased a single garbage truck and started his own garbage hauling business. He eventually built Waste Management, a national megamillion-dollar garbage hauling corporation. Then, in the early 1990s, Huizenga turned nineteen video rental stores into the industry leader, Blockbuster Video. He merged it with entertainment giant Viacom, creating a multibillion-dollar entertainment conglomerate.

How did Huizenga do it? In *The Making of a Blockbuster,* author Gail DeGeorge shares explanations from Huizenga's business partners. DeGeorge quotes one of Huizenga's partners, Steve Berrard, recounting how Huizenga would often start negotiations by discussing unrelated issues with opponents. Berrard goes on to say, "In [fifteen] minutes instead of holding on to the end of the table waiting to start haggling . . . they're the best of friends, they'd share, 'yeah, I was there, did you ever go here?'" Huizenga had apparently learned the value—and mastered the skills—of building rapport.

The necessity for good rapport is unquestionable. Just ask some people in Atlantic City, New Jersey. The city and many of its residents rely on casino gambling to fuel the economy there. But in 1999, unhappy with proposed pay raises, the union representing more than one-third of the city's work-force prepared for a strike. A previous strike in the mid-1980s had report-edly resulted in violence, property damage, and arrests. City leaders wor-ried that it could happen again. Casino operators were facing serious financial losses, and the city police faced the potentially difficult task of keep-ing the peace among thousands of striking workers.

This time, however, the negotiations between the union and casinos were heading in a different direction. This is what union president Robert McDevitt told news reporters, as printed in the *Atlantic City Press* August 20, 1999: "It's not a negative negotiation. My whole point has been to de-velop a relationship with the casino industry. It's certainly making the nego-tiating a lot easier. There's trust involved."

The cordial atmosphere of the negotiation was a safe bet. Workers did strike, but only for a few days, before the two sides reached an agreement. Police received no reports of violence and made no arrests.

When your opponents know that your empathy and understanding for them are intact, they are more willing to make concessions and negotiate harmoniously toward an agreement. The language you use to convey this message makes the difference. Use phrases such as: **"I know this issue means a lot to you, and I appreciate your willingness to discuss this with me,"** or **"If anyone can work out a fair deal here, I know that you're the person to do it."**

Good rapport between negotiators establishes the framework needed for a successful negotiation in the following ways. Rapport:

- helps you understand your opponent's feelings and beliefs.

- creates a positive atmosphere among the negotiators.

- reduces tension over the issues being negotiated.

- encourages openness and a willingness to discuss the issues clearly.

- makes negotiating easier and more enjoyable.

The level of rapport you need with an opponent depends on the type of deal. For example, you may find little need to create a lasting personal relationship with a salesman when you're purchasing a television. A few minutes of conversation and getting to know one another usually builds enough rapport to negotiate effectively in small deals. When dealing with someone you've already known for a while, common pleasantries like the following help reinforce your relationship: **"You look great today," "It's great to see you," "I'm glad we had a chance to get together and discuss this."**

At the other end of the spectrum, a corporate buyer may take months or years building rapport with a supplier with whom he or she expects to negotiate on a regular basis. In a merger of two major corporations, opponents are compelled to understand one another more thoroughly, seeking unanimity in their business philosophies, values, and goals. In building rapport for more formal scenarios you can use comments such as: **"I know you're a tough negotiator, but I admire your willingness to listen and be fair."**

What if you really dislike your opponent? That's OK. Nobody's suggesting you should fall in love with every opponent. But being polite and courteous is enough to keep the negotiation alive. Your goal is to convert your opponent to your way of thinking, not to conquer him or her.

The Process of Building Rapport

Understanding Your Opponent's Point of View

In 1959 Richard Nixon was planning his trip to meet with Soviet leader Nikita Khrushchev. Media pundits were saying that Nixon's mission during the trip should be to convince Khrushchev that America was for peace. Before heading to Moscow, Nixon reportedly sought advice from a friend, who told him this:

"There's no need to convince Khrushchev that America wants peace. He already knows we want peace. Your job is to convince the Soviet leader that he cannot win a war against America." Nixon learned that he needed to understand his opponent's point of view if he wanted to negotiate effectively.

Understanding your opponent's point of view means taking a sincere interest in him. Engage your opponent in conversation. Actively listen not only to what your opponent is saying, but also to what he is not saying. Ask your opponent to clarify his point of view. Paraphrase comments that your opponent makes and repeat them back. To illustrate:

Customer: "I don't like the whole-life insurance because it's more costly up front."

Salesperson: "So it's the short-term cost that concerns you."

This type of active listening encourages your opponent to clarify his or her point. This way you'll be able to examine the deeper meaning of your opponent's words. For example, if your opponent says she is looking for the "best deal," you'll be able to determine if "best deal" means either the lowest price or outstanding service.

Reveal Perceptions

We all have our own perceptions of issues we face. Work hard at understanding your opponent's perceptions and compare them with your own.

A developer I know ran into trouble because of a mix-up in perceptions. The local county government required that he plant trees around a newly planned commercial real estate development. The project was very large, and the developer's cost estimate for the trees exceeded his budget by nearly one hundred thousand dollars.

Hoping to avoid the unexpected cost, the developer argued with the county. At one point, a county official was so offended by the developer's aggressive approach that he considered delaying a permit. That would have driven costs even higher.

One day I asked the developer about his problem. "Exactly what kind of trees is the county requiring you to plant?" I asked.

"I don't know," he replied.

"Well, it might be worth it to ask them exactly what type of trees they expect," I suggested.

He did. And he learned that he had gone through all that trouble because he had perceived "trees" as large, mature, expensive trees, not the small, inexpensive saplings the county required.

 Ask your opponent to explain his or her perception of the issue being negotiated.

Too many times, negotiators get caught up in thinking of what they're going to say instead of listening closely to people's points of view and perceptions. Former U.S. Secretary of State Dean Rusk reportedly offered this solution: "One of the best ways to persuade others is with your ears—by listening to them."

The circumstances and experiences in our lives help create our perceptions. It's important to get to know as much as possible about your opponent's history. In your conversations you want to find common ground with your opponent. Search for the similarities in your lives. Examine how your opponent's circumstances, such as the following, can affect the negotiation.

Family/Personal Life

Have an interest in your opponent's family. Will your opponent's spouse or partner be an outside force in the negotiation? Is the marriage intact? Will a pending divorce affect the negotiation? Does your opponent have children? Will the children play a role in your opponent's decisions? In some cases you'll also want to learn about your opponent's personal interests (e.g., theater, art, movies, hobbies, education).

You may share mutual friends or be acquainted with a sibling. Knowing the same people could help you establish trust with your opponent. Learn who your opponent's friends are, whom they work with, and how your opponent's friends and family members may affect his or her decision-making.

Professional Life

How many times have you changed your career or workplace? Every time you changed, you met a new group of people and learned new skills. Your work experience could give you rapport-building information. You never know when you and an opponent might have shared the same line of work.

Personality Traits

The science of identifying human personality types has spawned numerous research materials and books. They explain in detail the basic personality types. You don't have to be an expert on the intricacies of human personality types to be an effective negotiator. However, it's helpful to recognize the obvious personality traits of your opponents. Are they passive or aggressive? Do they have a sense of humor, or are they serious? Are they outgoing and fond of compliments, or shy and quiet, preferring not to be the center of attention? Do they seem patient and willing to talk openly, or are they impatient and unwilling to reveal too much about themselves?

Understanding your opponent's personality will also help you discern how your opponent prefers to be treated. Someone who seeks recognition may like compliments. A person who appears authoritative may not be interested in small talk and will want to get to the bottom line quickly.

Adjust your negotiation style to match your opponent's personality.

It's also important to reveal your own personality without giving away your goal. If you share a mutual interest in tennis, you want to let your opponent know about it. You want to express your passion for the game. But if you were negotiating the price of a tennis racket with the same person, you wouldn't want to seem so enthusiastic that your opponent would recognize your immediate need for the racket as a weakness. Avoid giving your opponent information about your negotiating strategy before you're ready to move toward an agreement. Even the Old Testament makes this point:

"A fool uttereth all his mind; but a wise man keeps it until afterwards."
Proverbs 29:11

Cultural and Gender Differences

When you share cultural backgrounds and family traditions, rapport already exists. Use such an opportunity to build trust immediately. If your backgrounds are different, take the time to appreciate your opponent's culture.

Cultures can mean ethnic background or a particular lifestyle in general. For example, in the United States, some people think of themselves as "traditional" Americans. They are family oriented, conservative with their finances, and churchgoing. Other Americans concern themselves with status. Not only do they seek wealth, they want others to know they have it. Still other Americans prefer so-called alternative lifestyles. People typically take their different cultures seriously—you should take them seriously too.

When dealing with a person of the opposite sex, take into consideration the unfortunate existence of stereotypes. Some men perceive women as pushovers. Some women perceive men as condescending. Regardless of the reasons, these and other stereotypes persist. Be aware of them, and make the extra effort to show your opponent of the opposite sex that you plan to negotiate a fair and equitable agreement. We discuss this issue more in depth in Chapter Ten, "How to Negotiate with the Opposite Sex."

Be sensitive to cultural and gender differences.

Emotional State

Whether you've known your opponent for a long time or have just met him, understanding his emotions and controlling your own could make the difference between an easy and a difficult negotiation.

People often allow their emotions to get the best of them, especially while resolving conflict. Let's face it: anger is a natural emotion. But you don't have to give in to your emotions. People make the choice to become angry. They use their tempers to intimidate people into accepting their views. That's poor negotiating.

As we saw in Chapter One, if you can control your emotional behavior, you can negotiate in a controlled, conscious process that moves toward an agreement. Take this advice from Thomas Jefferson: "Nothing gives one person so much advantage over another as to remain cool and unruffled under all circumstances."

Emotions are ingrained in our minds, and they surface when something like a word, attitude, or event triggers them. Because emotions are so unpredictable, learning the cause of your opponent's emotions right away could save you trouble later in the negotiation.

If your opponent is feeling ill, stressed, or irritable over an issue other than the one you're negotiating, those negative feelings could spill over into your negotiation—many times in the form of anger. Take the following steps when your opponent's negative emotions are threatening a potential deal:

1. Assess the cause of the emotion. People often displace anger, meaning that they become upset with one person but take it out on someone else. A boss who's angry at his employees could go home in a bad mood and yell at his children over something as minor as talking too long on the telephone. A longtime business client could argue with his salesperson over price when the client is really upset over receiving poor service from the shipping department.

Sometimes opponents may become angry with you if they don't understand you. They may think you're trying to cheat them.

Assess the cause of the emotion early on by asking your opponent to talk about his or her feelings. You might say: **"You seem to have some concerns. What are they?"**

What if your opponent is unwilling to vent his or her frustrations? Sometimes, if time is not of the essence, postponing the negotiation is the best alternative.

Assess the cause of your opponent's emotions.

2. Identify coexisting emotions. People often experience several emotions at one time. A mother could experience extreme anxiety or fear when her teenage son isn't home by the required time. She might worry that something bad has happened to him. Then, once the teenager arrives home an hour or two late, the mother might express anger by scolding her son and punishing him. In such a case, the mother would be expressing her fear and anxiety in the form of anger.

If your opponent becomes upset during the negotiation, defuse his or her concerns by assuring your opponent that you understand those concerns, and that you plan to address them during the negotiation. Use comments like: **"My intent was not to upset you,"** or **"The last thing I want to do is make you angry."**

Negative emotions may just be a bump in the road instead of a barrier in the negotiation. In fact, listening sympathetically can become a rapport-building exercise.

Help overcome your opponent's negative emotions with a sympathetic ear. Allow your opponent to vent.

3. Use consequential thinking. The best negotiators consider the consequences of their opponents' negative emotional reactions, and they share those consequences with their opponents. The following story will help illustrate this point:

An executive at a television station became concerned when the news director consistently arrived late for weekly management meetings. The executive privately and calmly pointed out to the news director that he was making note of the problem in the news director's employment file. In response, the news director lashed out, criticizing the station's policy on management meetings and complaining that he didn't get paid to attend "stupid" meetings.

Instead of reacting negatively to the news director's emotional outburst, the executive first explained that he understood the man's frustration. He then explained that the news director's negative behavior could damage their working relationship and cause friction among other workers at the station.

The executive did not try to override the news director's emotions with logical reasons. He simply stated the potential consequences of the negative emotional behavior. The executive, at some point, would have to discuss the logical reasons, but it would be most effective to wait until the emotions had subsided.

When people clearly understand the consequences of their negative behavior, chances are better that they will see a more reasonable method of solving the problem.

 Use consequential thinking when responding to negative emotions.

Researching Your Opponent

"You have one of the best cases I've ever come across in my law career. I want to help you," exclaimed the lawyer.

"Thank you," said the man. "But I have to go now." He grabbed his hat and coat and almost ran toward the door.

"What's wrong? I told you that you could win this case. Why are you leaving?" asked the lawyer.

"Well," said the man, "I think I'll be better off settling this case out of court."

"But I just told you, it's a great case. You can't lose."

"Oh, yes, I can," said the man. "Because what I just told you was my opponent's side of the story."

That's one clever way to research your opponent.

Like building rapport, researching your opponent could require only minutes, or it could take weeks to accomplish. It all depends on the type of negotiation. Researching your opponent may also occur simultaneously with building rapport. How does researching your opponent help in your negotiation?

- You unmask your opponent's goal.

- You determine your opponent's strengths and weaknesses.

- You discover your opponent's hot buttons.

- You test your opponent's negotiating style.

Unmask Your Opponent's Goal

During a reelection campaign, one political candidate for state office in California was asked about his stance on the issue of casino gambling. The politician knew that only half of his constituents approved of gambling. So he replied, "If you mean the wretched evil which tears apart husbands and wives, takes food away from little children, and leads countless victims to the depths of despair, then I'm against it. But if, by casino gambling, you're talking about the excitement of chance, a revitalized economy, and the source of tax dollars that could help us build a hospital for the sick and give food to the needy, then certainly I'm for it. That is my unyielding position on this issue."

If you were negotiating with this politician over the issue of gambling, would you know what his real goal was? The politician told his constituents on both sides of the issue what they wanted to hear. But he never revealed his personal feelings. Let's face it. He was trying to appease both sides in hopes of being reelected.

Sometimes people will limit what they tell you, or they'll tell you what they think you want to hear instead of what you really need to know. One way to overcome this problem is by asking open-ended questions. Get your opponents to elaborate on their thoughts and feelings.

You don't want to come off as a news reporter, asking hard, penetrating questions. Instead, you should pose questions as part of your friendly conversation. But it's a good idea to think like a reporter, seeking answers to the proverbial *who, what, where, when, why,* and *how* questions.

Another effective way of unmasking the goal is to ask your opponent for advice about aspects of the issue being negotiated. Lay out the challenge you're facing, and ask your opponent how he feels about it. In the case of the California politician, you would want to seek his advice by asking a question something like this: **"What type of legislation do you believe could allow California to generate tax dollars from gambling and, at the same time, prevent it from hurting people?"**

One way to unmask your opponent's goal is by asking for his or her advice on aspects of the issue being negotiated.

Determine Strengths and Weaknesses

Journalist and author David Brinkley, in his book *Washington Goes to War*, tells an amusing story about negotiating strengths and weaknesses. Brinkley explains how in 1938 President Franklin D. Roosevelt revealed plans for a new project that caused an uproar among many people in Washington D.C. Roosevelt wanted to build a new memorial for Thomas Jefferson on land occupied by Washington's cherished Japanese cherry trees. The construction meant the trees would be destroyed.

When the bulldozers arrived, Brinkley writes, protesters chained themselves to the trees, challenging the construction workers. In response, one of Roosevelt's advisers ordered that the protesters be served lunch and as many cups of coffee as they could drink. Eventually the protesters had to unlock their chains and leave for the rest rooms. Construction of the memorial went on as planned.

Roosevelt's adviser recognized a weakness in the protesters' negotiating strategy. We all have weaknesses going into our negotiations. And we all deal from strengths as well. It's crucial that you determine both the strengths and weaknesses of your opponents before the negotiating begins.

Examine your strengths and weaknesses and those of your opponent.

A simple example of strength is a person's experience or sophistication level regarding the issue under negotiation. A lack of understanding is a weakness.

People with whom you negotiate will show a variety of strengths and weaknesses at the same time. Consider the following two case studies to help you understand this point:

The case of the stereo salesman:

One of the salesman's strengths is his extensive knowledge of the stereo systems he sells. He has the ability to promote the benefits of his products. But he could, at the same time, show weakness if he doesn't know the products and prices that his competitors are offering.

As a buyer, you could negotiate with the salesman's weakness in mind. By learning about stereos and what products and prices the salesman's competitors are offering, you can make an informed decision on what to offer for a new stereo. You could also say to the salesman: **"I've shopped your competitors, and I'm wondering if you can do better on the price."**

The case of the overworked employee:

A secretary has worked in the same law firm for more than five years. She never misses work, and she has become the most proficient clerical worker in the office. For her loyalty, the secretary is motivated to seek a pay raise.

The secretary knows her boss's weaknesses. She believes that he will do whatever he can to avoid confrontation with employees. Sometimes he even comes off as a pushover when employees ask for favors. This knowledge serves as a strength for the secretary. However, in her research of the market, she learns that the raise she is seeking far exceeds the market's top pay for her position. The secretary's weakness is her unrealistic expectation.

Discover Your Opponent's Hot Buttons

Hot buttons are topics that people get passionate about. People commonly refer to their hot buttons repeatedly and express either their positive or negative feelings about them. As you eventually move toward an agreement, you can use hot buttons as tools in persuading your opponent.

Your opponent's responses to your questions may unveil his or her hot buttons.

Test Your Opponent's Negotiating Style

Our negotiating styles usually emerge from our individual mind-sets. As we examined earlier, negotiating styles range from "tender" to "tough." Tender negotiators avoid conflict at all cost. Tough negotiators appear stubborn, and are generally unafraid of conflict. The most successful negotiators are flexible, adapting their style between tender and tough.

One way to test your opponent's negotiating style is by offering a story about a negotiation that you've experienced. The manner in which your opponent reacts to the story may reveal his or her style. To further illustrate:

If you had a bad experience with a carpet cleaning company and felt you paid too much and received poor service, you could explain the situation to your opponent in general conversation. If he responds by saying something like "You should have stopped payment on the check and taken the jerk to small claims court!" he likely uses a tough negotiating style.

Another way of testing an opponent's negotiating style is to ask "what if" questions. If you're negotiating with the owner of an auto repair shop, ask: **"What if I chose to have more than just my brakes repaired. What is the discount?"** Whether you wanted more repairs or not wouldn't matter. Your goal would be to elicit a response that could reveal your opponent's style.

Test your opponent's negotiating style.

Two Hurdles That Make Negotiations Difficult

Egoism

A person's ego, when pervasive, is the toughest hurdle of all to overcome in a negotiation. Egoism keeps people from reaching an agreement for the most unreasonable of reasons. It can rule the negotiation process because it leads people to believe that only their interests really matter. If you recognize that your opponent is an egomaniac, take on a tender negotiating style. Avoid overtly disagreeing with or contradicting the person. It'll hurt his or her pride. Political author Christopher Matthews once said, "Focusing on your own ego is a guarantee of failure. The smart politician never takes his eyes off the other fellow's ego."

Keep your ego in check. And keep an eye on your opponent's ego.

Poor Communication and Mixed Signals

In 1942, American Civil Defense authorities reportedly printed posters announcing that wartime blackouts were needed to save energy. The posters read, "Illumination must be extinguished when premises are vacated." If the authorities had used plain English to communicate more effectively, the posters would have read, "Turn out the lights when you leave." Sometimes people make communication difficult.

Have you ever been in a conversation that ended with your still not understanding what the other person was talking about? A total communication breakdown like this may prove difficult to rebuild. The culprits—poor communicators—usually create barriers because either they don't express themselves skillfully or they don't listen. Too many people spend time thinking of what to say next instead of listening.

If you're dealing with a poor communicator, actively listen. When you don't get a reasonable answer to your question, ask it again in a different way. Furthermore, know exactly what you want to communicate. Speak clearly with succinct and concise sentences. Poor communication can lead to mixed-up perceptions among opponents. Consider the following examples of mixed perceptions:

A negotiation involving Catherine the employer and Joe the employee:

> Employee: "Catherine hasn't been a good boss. She never gives me the direction that I need, and she never shares any feedback on my work."

> Employer: "I give Joe a lot of freedom. I leave him alone and let him do his job without any interference from me."

A negotiation between a used-car salesman and a customer:

> Salesman: "This car is in great shape for a ten-year-old car. It looks like the owner kept it in a garage for ten years. What a great buy!"

> Customer: "A ten-year-old car? I can already see the repair bills stacking up!"

Can you see how perceptions vary when communication is lacking?

Summary

- Your opponent is anyone with whom you are attempting to reach an agreement.

- Don't confuse your opponent with the issue.

- Yield to your opponent. Let the person speak so you can clearly understand his or her point of view.

- Avoid the "us against them" attitude.

- Don't jump to conclusions.

- Take the time to create a positive environment in which to negotiate.

⏱ **Alienation is the enemy of a successful negotiation.**

⏱ **Not only is it wrong to prejudge people or have biases against them, it's a mistake that usually has costly consequences.**

⏱ **Invest time in learning who the decision-maker is.**

⏱ **Stop yourself from jumping right into the negotiation. Build rapport first.**

⏱ **Ask your opponent to explain his or her perception of the issue being negotiated.**

⏱ **Adjust your negotiation style to match your opponent's personality.**

⏱ **Be sensitive to cultural and gender differences.**

⏱ **Assess the cause of your opponent's emotions.**

⏱ **Help overcome your opponent's negative emotions with a sympathetic ear. Allow your opponent to vent.**

⏱ **Use consequential thinking when responding to negative emotions.**

⏱ **One way to unmask your opponent's goal is by asking for his or her advice on aspects of the issue being negotiated.**

⏱ **Examine your strengths and weaknesses and those of your opponent.**

⏱ **Your opponent's responses to your questions may unveil his or her hot buttons.**

⏱ **Test your opponent's negotiating style.**

⏱ **Keep your ego in check. And keep an eye on your opponent's ego.**

CHAPTER FIVE

Step 2:
Understand the Challenge

The Big Picture

As January 1981 drew closer, fifty-three American hostages faced another New Year's Day in the custody of their Islamic revolutionary captors. Fourteen months earlier, a militant group of Iranians had stormed the U.S. embassy in Tehran and taken these American workers hostage. But this new year offered real hope for the hostages, their families, and the American people. The hostage crisis in Iran was finally coming to an end. After Ronald Reagan had won the presidential election over Jimmy Carter, word came from the Iranian captors that they would release the hostages once Reagan took the oath of office and Carter moved out of the White House.

Jimmy Carter and his officials had made several unsuccessful attempts to negotiate a release of the hostages before 1981. Why did they fail? Was there an obstacle that hindered Carter's ability to negotiate successfully with the Iranians?

Several of the Iranian captors spoke openly to news reporters about the crisis years later. They explained that Carter had faced at least one almost insurmountable challenge. Many Iranians considered Carter an enemy of their country because he had built an alliance with the longtime leader of Iran, Muhammad Reza Pahlavi, better known as the Shah of Iran. In 1979, Iranian revolutionaries overthrew the Shah, labeled him an enemy of Iran, and forced him to flee the country. Since Carter had supported the Shah's government, the revolutionaries also considered Carter an enemy. And the militant captors vowed never to give in to Carter.

The American hostage crisis in Iran embodied a variety of complex issues that only experts on international affairs could expound upon. But a simple lesson on negotiation arose out of the crisis—that we must clearly understand the challenges facing us if we want to find success in our negotiations.

No matter what you call them—obstacles, hurdles, problems, or dilemmas—they all challenge your potential for reaching an agreement. That's why this step is called "**Understand the Challenge**." The "challenge" is either one obstacle or a collection of obstacles that pose a threat to reaching a satisfying agreement.

The INSTANT NEGOTIATOR system takes an approach based on aggressively attacking challenges while patiently empathizing with people. In order to attack the challenge in a negotiation, you must first identify it. But understanding the challenge means more than simply recognizing the obvious hurdles. You must look beneath the obvious and search for hidden obstacles, then analyze the effect each obstacle may have on your ability to make a fair deal. In essence, understanding the challenge is contemplating the "big picture" of a negotiation.

Contemplate the big picture
of a negotiation.

Hidden Challenges

Until 1920 it's reported that no Westerner had ever witnessed the awesome majesty of Nepal's Mount Everest from closer than forty miles away. Yet the world's tallest mountain captivated the curiosity of adventurers. In a 1924 expedition, mountain climbers from the United States and Great Britain faced several obstacles in their trek up Mount Everest. Bitter cold, blinding snow, and steep, icy cliffs offered climbers a formidable and exhausting challenge.

But another obstacle to reaching their goal was not so obvious to their eyes and ears. When Howard Summerville climbed nearly twenty-seven thousand feet up the face of the mountain, the concealed challenge emerged: It was the thinning, air that, at such a high altitude, made breathing almost impossible. Summerville, nearly suffocating from lack of oxygen, failed in his struggle for the summit. He succeeded later in a second attempt.

Just as the freezing, treacherous weather conditions posed an obvious challenge to the Mount Everest climbers, the challenges in our negotiations also may appear obvious and simple to understand. But like the thin air that threatened the life of Howard Summerville, the real obstacles in our negotiations often are hidden—and they can prove most detrimental.

What you don't see in a negotiation can hurt you. Hidden obstacles frequently emerge too late for many negotiators to defend against. Like a ship sailing toward an iceberg, you can clearly see the obvious challenge and figure out how to avoid it. But beneath the surface of that challenge often lies a larger, more complicated obstacle. So, if you don't want to get caught off guard in your negotiations, you must become an investigator of sorts, expecting and exposing the unforeseen challenges and finding the big picture of the negotiation.

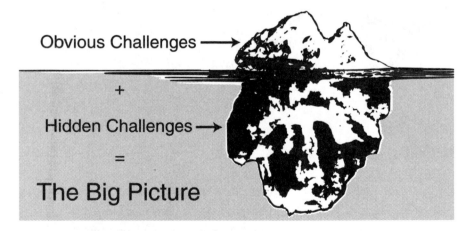

Obvious Challenges ⟶

\+

Hidden Challenges ⟶

\=

The Big Picture

Ask Revealing Questions

How do you investigate the challenge? By asking the right questions of your opponents! Your goal is to learn the underlying interests of your opponents by eliciting revealing answers to your questions.

I had an opportunity to test my questioning skills once while vacationing in the hills of North Carolina. I stopped in an antiques consignment shop and began building rapport with the storekeeper. After some initial pleasantries I asked, "So when I want to negotiate on the price of an item here, do I talk with the owner of the antique or do I negotiate with you?"

"I negotiate for the owners," replied the storekeeper.

My simple question revealed a significant obstacle—that I would have to deal with a middleman in the negotiation. Middlemen can hold firm on a price by using the seller as an excuse. For example, if I were negotiating over an item, the storekeeper could say, "The seller won't accept anything but full price for that item." There would be no way for me to know if his excuse was accurate. But my question also overcame part of that challenge. The storekeeper's answer ("I negotiate for the owners") disclosed that he was willing to move down on price.

Then I asked, "What limit do the owners give you when it comes to how much you can move down on price?"

The storekeeper answered, "Well, I have the authority to negotiate ten percent off the asking price." My second question revealed another obstacle. The storekeeper had a limit on how far he could move on the price. Once again, however, the question was so effective that I had already earned a ten-percent discount even before I picked something to buy. Can you see the importance of asking good questions?

Since each negotiation is unique, the questions you raise will also be unique. When you pose questions to your opponent, you should structure them so they extract thorough information from the person. Don't just seek the answers you want to hear in hopes the negotiation will be an easy task. Keep an open mind, and ask with a sincere interest in learning about your opponent's needs.

Sometimes you'll simply raise questions for yourself to answer. This process works as a mental checklist. It helps you analyze what you've learned from your opponent.

Consider the following sample questions you would want to ask yourself in these common scenarios, to help in your probe for the challenge:

Purchasing a Home at a Specific Price

What is the real value of the house?

The seller believes the house is worth one hundred-thousand-dollars. You want to buy the home, but you want to pay below market value. You research the value of the home by comparing sales of similar homes in the area, and you hire a professional real estate appraiser to evaluate the market value. Through this effort you learn that the real market value of the house is only ninety thousand dollars. Before any negotiating on the price has even begun, you and the seller already have a ten-thousand-dollar difference in your opinions of the home's real market value. Your challenge runs deeper than just negotiating a price below market value. The seller's unrealistic perception of the home's value is a more complex challenge.

What if you are the seller? At least one challenge is obvious. You would need to justify the high asking price.

How much demand exists for the house?

If several people want to purchase the home at the same time, such demand could leave the seller with no incentive to come down on the asking price. If the demand for the home is weak, the seller may be motivated to sell at a price lower than the initial asking price—or even below the real market value.

Are there any hidden facts?

The crime rate is an example of a hidden fact to a buyer. If the crime rate in the area is high, the buyer might have second thoughts about purchasing a home in that neighborhood. But if the seller has never personally been affected by crime, she might not consider the crime rate a factor in the desirability or value of the home.

What is motivating the other person?

Something is motivating the seller to sell and the buyer to buy. How high or how low is that motivation level? The seller might be highly motivated and willing to take a low offer. On the other hand, the seller may be willing to wait for the highest price possible. The buyer might have six months to search for a home, or he or she might move in a few weeks. Moreover, the buyer and seller may or may not be willing to negotiate on items other than price, such as including furniture, paying for the buyer's financing costs, or closing the deal in a desired time frame. Examining these issues can help you gauge the motivation level of the other person.

Why do personalities matter?

People's personalities clash once in a while. Other times they mesh perfectly. You'll want to explore your opponent's personality traits. Anyone who has been a real estate salesperson knows that deals can fall apart quickly when buyers and sellers don't like each other.

Make an unprejudiced assessment of your opponent's personality. Is the person friendly or shy, congenial or impatient, flexible or firm? Examine what the differences or similarities in your personalities will mean to the negotiation.

What effect does a "middleman" have in the negotiation?

Many home buyers never negotiate directly with sellers. Instead, they deal with a middleman such as a real estate agent. In these cases, understanding the challenge could require more of an effort. You'll need to research the middleman as well as the seller and understand his or her personality, motivation, and negotiating style (see "Researching Your Opponent," p. 56).

Can you see how exploring the answers to these questions gives you a deeper understanding of the challenge you face in each negotiation? Numerous factors other than price enter into the sale and purchase of a home.

Now take a look at how you can understand the challenge more clearly in another common negotiation:

Leasing or Buying a New Car

Can you justify the price?

When you're researching cars, you'll want to compare apples to apples when it comes to features and options. Prioritize the options you need compared with those you merely want, and determine which car is priced best based on the options most suitable for you. Salespeople often pitch a car's prestige, hoping the customer's ego will influence her to buy or lease an expensive model. You'll want to decide ahead of time what's most important to you—either driving around in an expensive vehicle or saving money by owning or leasing an average-priced car.

What is the value of your trade-in vehicle?

Before you begin discussing the price of a new car, you should first have the dealer commit to a firm price on your trade-in. The dealer obviously wants to give you as little money as possible on the trade-in so that he can make as large a profit as possible after it sells. Don't let the new car's low price dictate your decision. Get the best price on the trade-in even before you begin talking numbers on the new car. You can research the value of your trade-in by calling your local bank and asking for the value. You can also find the "blue book" value on the Internet.

What is the dealer cost vs. the sticker price?

Most people realize that they can make an offer on a new car lower than the sticker price. But how much lower is usually reasonable? The simple answer lies in the dealer's cost for the vehicle. So, instead of taking the sticker price and working down from there, find the dealer's cost for the vehicle and decide how much you're willing to pay above the dealer's cost. Many car-buying experts suggest that paying $300 to $500 above the dealer's cost is a reasonable offer. Keep in mind, however, that the dealer could pay even less than the invoice cost for the car if the manufacturer provides discounts that aren't typically disclosed.

Price is still a factor when you lease a car. Don't let the dealer talk only in terms of monthly lease payments. When you lease a car, you pay the difference between the price of the car and the predetermined or residual value of the car at the end of the lease—plus interest.

What is the residual value when leasing the car?

The "residual value" is the predetermined value of the car at the end of the lease. When you lease, you pay the difference between the price and the residual value, which is called the "depreciation" or the decrease in value of the car. The smaller the gap between the price and the residual value, the lower your monthly payment. You should negotiate to have the dealer increase the residual value. If his leasing finance company won't allow an increase, have the dealer research other finance companies who might offer a higher residual value.

Should you buy or lease?

There are no hard and fast rules for determining the best route for your situation. But you should consider a few factors. If you usually keep your cars for more than four years, and you're consistent with maintenance, you might be better off buying. After four years you probably have paid down your car loan enough so there's equity in the car. You can use that equity for a down payment when you purchase a new car.

Although leasing offers a smaller monthly payment for more car, you usually don't build equity in leased vehicles. Unlike buying, when the lease is over, you don't own the car. You have no equity to apply to your next car. If you trade in your car every two to three years, and you don't build equity anyway, leasing might fit your needs. In addition, if you use your car for business, you can deduct a large portion of the lease payment on your taxes.

When is the best time to lease a new car?

The residual value of a car drops as the model year progresses. So you're better off leasing at the start of the model year, when the cars first arrive. That's when their residual value is highest. Leasing a "leftover" at the end of the model year car is not always a good idea because the residual value will be considerably less.

How much time do you have to make a deal?

Salespeople invest valuable time in negotiating deals. They want to get paid something for their time. This factor gives you, the buyer, negotiating power. If you're patient and move slowly through the process, you have a better chance of negotiating a better deal for yourself. The salesperson doesn't have as much time as you do because she needs to close numerous sales to make a living.

What kind of financing options are available?

You'll want to compare the dealer's financing options with those offered by your local bank. Take a look at interest rates, terms, and the type of loan: Is it simple interest or "rule of 78" financing, where you pay all the interest up front? Interest rates and terms apply to leasing, too. You pay interest on top of the "depreciation." Sometimes finance companies will offer lower interest rates if you accept a shorter lease term.

Negotiating Over a Raise

What's the real value of the position?

A middle manager at a computer manufacturing company learns that her company is launching a new high-tech assembly line system. It will eliminate the need for any new assembly line workers and management. The manager's position is safe, but the company will limit her duties. In seeking a raise, the manager must examine closely what she is being paid for and how valuable her position is to the employer now that her job duties are limited. The manager should also objectively determine if her position warrants the type of salary she is seeking. Her opponent, the employer, would want to ask similar questions: Is the manager being overpaid for her limited duties? Has the manager proven to be a valued employee in the past?

Could the company benefit by replacing the manager?

The manager would also want to examine the possibility of her company replacing her with a less experienced manager instead of giving her a raise. It would be worth the effort to research how much additional cost the employer will incur in recruiting and training a person with less experience, and if that additional cost exceeds the raise she's requesting. Once again, the employer would want to consider similar questions. Can the company save money over the long term by hiring less experienced managers? How could the cost of hiring and training offset potential savings? Would losing the manager have a negative effect on other employees?

Does the manager have skills that go beyond the job title?

Knowing that her limited duties could also limit her pay scale, the manager should investigate her personal value to the company. Are her skills versatile and useful in other departments of the company? Has she documented her performance and accomplishments with the company? Does she have an advanced educational degree and training? Does she have a unique ability to motivate other workers and make them more productive? The employer could evaluate the potential value of expanding the manager's responsibilities.

Can the manager enhance the company's success?

The manager would want to explore how she can make her employer better understand her value. Can she offer to work flexible hours or weekends? Can she obtain additional training and expertise at her own expense? Are there any areas of the company lacking in productivity where she can provide direction? By the same token, the employer could explore how he can get more productivity out of the manager.

Are you now convinced that negotiating a raise entails more than just asking for more money? You should be! Your answers to questions like the ones I posed may give you a clearer understanding of the big picture and the challenge that lies ahead.

A Good Starting Point

Every negotiation holds its own unique problems that serve as the primary challenge. So the questions you raise for yourself to answer while exploring each problem will be specific to that particular negotiation. However, the following questions serve as an outline. They're versatile enough to use in almost any negotiation.

In these questions you might recognize the three negotiating fundamentals: time, power, and knowledge. Since they exist in almost every negotiation, you can use them as a starting point from which to seek solutions to problems.

- What is my opponent's TIME frame?
  What is my TIME frame?

- What is my opponent's POWER?
  What is my POWER?

- What is my opponent's KNOWLEDGE?
  What is my KNOWLEDGE?

Opposing and Mutual Interests as Challenges

In negotiation it's easy to be fooled by the appearance of opposing interests. Be aware of them, but delve deeper into the underlying meaning of a person's opposing interests. Consider the opposing interests of Ted and Mary, for example. Ted and Mary saved some extra money. Ted wanted to buy a new entertainment center for their house. Mary wanted to use the money for a family vacation in Yellowstone National Park.

Ted and Mary exhibited opposing interests as to how they should spend their money. Sounds like a simple difference of opinion—right? Well, consider these underlying pieces of the puzzle that Ted and Mary failed to explain to each other.

In the last year, the couple's busy schedules created a communication gap not only between themselves but also between them and their teenage son and daughter. Realizing the tension within the family, Ted assumed that a new entertainment center would give the family time together watching movies at home and enjoying each other's company. On the other hand, Mary believed that the family would be better served without the distraction of television, spending quiet time in the wilderness of Yellowstone National Park and creating a bond among the family members.

Can you see how deep the challenge goes here? It stretches far beyond a preference for television movies versus a preference for a vacation in Yellowstone. It relates more to the couple's mutual interest in preventing a breakdown in the family relationship. Ted and Mary didn't have opposing interests after all. In fact, they shared a mutual interest.

This example can apply to professional situations as well. Business partners may have different opinions on how to market their company. Managers could disagree on the best way to solve an employee conflict. Law partners could prefer different defense strategies for their client.

Behind an apparent opposing interest often lies a mutual interest, something that you and your opponent can use to build upon. The mutual interest between Ted and Mary was to keep harmony in the family. A mutual interest obligates people to continue talking. It motivates negotiators to seek satisfying agreements. But unless you're fully aware of the mutual interests, you may find yourself trapped within the confines of opposing interests and unable to fully understand the challenge.

Evaluating Potential Solutions

Many authors have written about identifying and understanding problems. Some experts on the subject, like the Reverend Dr. Robert Schuller, view problem identification and problem solving as a state of mind. The following quote was attributed to Dr. Schuller: "Problems are only decisions waiting to be made."

On the other hand, you have more skeptical thinkers, like Andy Rooney who is quoted as saying, "A lot of people assume that we live in an orderly world where every event has meaning and every problem has a solution. I suspect, however, that some events are meaningless and some problems insoluble." And there's the ever-worried Peanuts cartoon character Charlie Brown, who concluded, "No problem is so big that it can't be run away from!"

One theory on problem solving seems to ring true most often. That theory is what some people call "outside of the box" thinking. It suggests that a person should broaden his or her view of a problem by looking outside of the problem for a better understanding.

Confused? Here's a story that makes the point:

Residents of a new high-rise condominium building called on an engineer to speed up the building's elevators. Many residents complained of frustration while waiting long periods of time for the elevators. The engineer reviewed the situation and determined that the building needed another elevator shaft. But that would cost the condominium association a lot of money it didn't have. After seeking a deeper understanding of the residents' problem, he found an ingenious solution. The engineer installed mirrors around the elevators on every floor. People became so preoccupied with looking at themselves or at others in the mirrors that they forgot about the wait. The engineer thought "outside of the box."

What if you don't consider yourself a creative thinker? Seek advice from someone who is creative. Ask your creative adviser for tips on how to think up ideas. For some people, creative thinking is more than just thinking. It's an active process of exploring for ideas. We'll discuss the process of producing ideas in Chapter Six, "Step 3: Introduce New Alternatives."

Understanding Perceptions

Challenges are often as complex as the perception one has of them. When someone tells you something, you accept that information based on your own perceptions. The difference in perceptions may cause you to misunderstand the motives of the person who communicated the information.

An example of different perceptions is the problem between business partners in a restaurant arguing over whether to keep the front door of the restaurant open.

Partner A says, "Customers will hate that draft coming through the door." Partner B says, "Customers will love to feel the cool breeze." One calls it a *draft*, and the other calls it a *breeze*—two different perceptions over the same issue.

If someone says to you in a negotiation, "If you don't reduce the price by ten percent, I'm going to have to use your competitor," what perception would you have of that comment? You might perceive that the opponent simply is looking for the lowest price. But maybe the opponent wants to buy from you and is looking for more value. You can't know unless you ask. A possible question is: **"Are you getting the same quality of service from**

the competitor that I can offer?" This question will lead to further discussion that helps you understand perceptions more clearly.

Understanding perceptions takes some self-reflection. It requires you to stop and think about why a person is communicating certain information and what meaning you have given to that information. Be honest with yourself about your feelings, and about how your personality interprets the information.

In negotiating conflicts, you can change an opponent's perception of an issue by redefining or renaming the conflict. A divorce situation provides an example:

A husband might say, "I'm not going to give in to her on the custody of the children." The husband perceives the issue as a problem between his wife and himself. But the issue could be redefined this way: "What is in the best interests of the children?" This question changes the conflict from a "him against her" battle into the task of finding a mutually acceptable solution.

Do You Really Want the Same Thing?

A commercial real estate investor named Victoria was interested in buying a small shopping center from another investor named Harold. Harold advertised the property for $500,000. Victoria submitted a contract for $460,000, a reasonable offer. Although Victoria and Harold initiated their negotiation based on the obvious difference in price, their underlying issues made the deal more complex. Harold needed money to pay his back taxes and wanted to close the deal within a few weeks. Victoria needed three months to close on a property she was selling. She also needed time to seek financing for the shopping center.

These underlying issues played a significant role in the negotiation. Harold had limited time. Victoria needed more time. Harold felt pressure to pay his taxes. Victoria felt the pressure of trying to successfully close the other sale and find financing. Despite the underlying issues, Victoria and Harold spent more time focusing on the difference in price. They counteroffered back and forth several times over a period of two weeks.

Finally Victoria and Harold both began to realize the importance of their underlying issues, and entered them into the negotiation. In a matter of days, they agreed on a price of $473,000. But more importantly, they also agreed to use Victoria's escrow money to pay part of Harold's back taxes, which were due immediately. And Victoria obtained a bridge loan on her other property which provided her the money to close on the shopping center a few weeks earlier. Their creative resolution in the deal finally came from their understanding of the underlying issues.

Can you see how the obvious issue can take a back seat to underlying issues? Even though people may seem to negotiate over the same issue, they will often pursue more vigorous efforts to satisfy their underlying wants and needs.

Underlying issues often arise in personal relationships. Consider Nick and Tammy, a husband and wife negotiating on where to go on vacation. They eventually agreed on a trip to Hawaii. But after they arrived, Nick wanted only to relax on the beach and read novels. Tammy wanted to go surfing and deep-sea diving. Conflict arose over their different wants. The couple had negotiated on the same issue—a vacation in Hawaii. But they never fully explored what each person wanted to do in Hawaii. Nick and Tammy didn't understand the real challenge in their negotiation. Both ended up dissatisfied as a result.

 Seek a deeper understanding of the challenge by exploring underlying issues.

Do You Really Know What Your Opponent Wants?

Now that you know how challenges may appear simpler than they really are, take a look at how solutions are just as tricky. Consider the story of the man who walks into a doctor's office with a chicken on his head.

The surprised doctor asks, "Uh, may I help you?"

"Yes," says the chicken, "I was hoping you could get this guy out from under me!"

That's an old joke, but it makes a timeless point. We should all avoid blindly assuming that we know exactly what our opponent wants.

People shouldn't be afraid to make assumptions. It's when we think all our assumptions are fact that we can end up looking foolish. There's an old tale about a U.S. Navy commander who assumed once too often. He was with his fleet on the high seas. A light appeared in the distance directly in the way of the fleet. So the admiral gave his radioman the order, "Warn that ship's people that they must change course fifteen degrees west, and let them know we're the U.S. Navy."

The radioman made the call, and the word came back. "Navy vessel, change your course fifteen degrees west."

That response infuriated the admiral. He grabbed the radio and firmly stated, "I order you to change *your* course fifteen degrees west, sir. I am an admiral in the U.S. Navy and I am standing on the most powerful battleship in the world, so you'd better move!"

A message came back, "I'm impressed with your rank in the Navy, sir, but you better change *your* course fifteen degrees west, because I'm an employee of the state park service, and right now I'm standing in a lighthouse."

If you assume something when preparing to negotiate, remind yourself that it's only an assumption, and be sure to thoroughly investigate it.

It's dangerous to think your assumptions are the facts.

Active Listening to Understand the Challenge

Active listening plays a crucial role in our ability to understand the challenge. But active listening is not an inborn ability. It's a skill that must be learned, and a difficult one at that.

In our personal lives, active listening leads to more caring and loving relationships. It tells a person that you're making an effort to understand his or her point of view. When people in the business world perfect their listening skills, they work more efficiently, production increases, and the workplace atmosphere becomes friendlier.

Poor listening, on the other hand, creates miscommunication and arguments, and in marriages often leads to divorce. When listening suffers, so does business. Clients can be made to feel unimportant, and employees or coworkers can feel unappreciated.

Someone once said, "I think I'll learn more from listening. Anything I would say I already know."

Listen actively—so your opponents know they've been heard.

Active listening means openly analyzing your opponent's dialogue, questioning in a positive way what people say and why and how they say it. You'll want to offer feedback like: **"Tell me why you feel that way,"** or **"If I'm hearing you correctly you said…"**

By paraphrasing statements you let the person know that you're making an effort to understand her interests as clearly as possible. You're also encouraging the person to continue making the point.

Active listening also requires sincere body language on your part, such as eye contact, head nodding, and facial expressions. You should refrain from thinking up responses. Keep your mind open and focused on accepting information. Once you fully comprehend the information, forming your responses becomes easier. If you understand the information, let your opponent know you understand. Show respect for your opponent's opinion.

When you disagree with your opponent, you might be tempted to express your disagreement or defend a position. Don't! You'll have an opportunity to state your case later. At this point you're gathering data. You're not in the intensive stage of the negotiation yet.

Disagreement is not the same as disapproval. Disagreement pertains to the facts of the situation. Disapproval is your evaluation of the person. Make sure you know whether you're feeling disagreement or disapproval when you're trying to understand the challenge.

Instead of expressing your disagreement, simply let your opponent know you understand his or her point of view.

Avoid misleading your opponent by saying you agree with the facts if you really don't. That's a crucial mistake that could come back to haunt you. In some cases, you might *not* want your opponent to know you agree with him. You can use your agreement as a concession or bargaining chip later.

As you gather information, prioritize your opponent's interests. Write them down on paper if you have the time. Make sure you prioritize the interests based on how your opponent sees his own interests, not based on how you see yours.

Have you ever noticed how people are more willing to listen intently to what you have to say only after you've listened to them first? That happens because people who feel understood are willing to return the favor. This opens the door for you to begin "planting seeds" in your opponent's mind about your point of view.

People have a natural tendency to reject points of view that they feel are forced upon them. But when you gradually, gently, present your ideas, a little at a time, you allow your opponent to interpret the information slowly and become comfortable with it over time.

Saint Thomas Aquinas might have recognized the significance of this point more than anyone. Aquinas is reported to have said, "When you want to convert someone to your view, you go over to where he is standing, take him by the hand, and guide him. You don't stand across the room and shout at him; you don't order him to come over to where you are. You start where he is, and work from that position."

Aquinas was obviously speaking figuratively when he talked about "taking someone by the hand." Another figurative way to look at this stage of the pre-negotiation process is to picture the discussion as a courteous tennis match in which the ball is volleyed back and forth softly and directly between the players. No kill shots! Just soft volleying—with empathy, understanding, and sincerity.

Present your point of view gently and carefully so your opponent has time to become comfortable with it.

Stay open-minded, even if you think you understand the challenge. Things change. Have you ever changed your mind? People change their minds from time to time on how they feel about issues, especially as they learn more facts.

The late U.S. Senator Everett M. Dirksen reportedly said about changing his mind, "I am a man of fixed and unbending principles, the first of which is to be flexible at all times."

Keep an open mind.
Realize that the challenge
can change from time to time.

Human Needs and Emotional Responses

Former U.S. Senator Vance Hartke was once quoted as saying, "Wars are . . . often the product of the conflicting intentions of decent men who have lost the patience to negotiate." Although Hartke made a valuable point, you can take his theory one step further. Wars happen when decent people feel that their basic human needs are threatened. If people feel threatened, hostility is almost assured, and the negotiation will most likely break down.

Experts on human behavior have categorized human needs in numerous ways. But no matter what scientific jargon you use for human needs, they all boil down to the basics: food, shelter, love, security, well-being (economic and emotional), and feeling important. I'll restate the last as a need: "the need to feel important."

Dale Carnegie wrote a lot about people craving importance. In his renowned book, *How to Win Friends and Influence People,* Carnegie establishes that the need to feel important is "a longing almost as deep, almost as imperious as the desire for food . . . which is seldom gratified." Carnegie also says, "This desire makes you want to wear the latest styles, drive the latest car, and talk about your brilliant children."

What does this mean in negotiation? People negotiate with their own importance in mind. They also want you to recognize that they are worthwhile. Do it! Give your opponent sincere appreciation. Avoid saying things in a way that could wound a person's pride.

Our Emotions

Emotional responses from your opponents can pose perplexing challenges in your negotiations. You cannot always know exactly how the other person is feeling. Moreover, what seems rational to your opponent might not seem rational to you, and vice versa.

In Chapter Four, "Step 1: Know Your Opponent," we discussed the ways to assess emotions. In this step, part of understanding the challenge is to grasp the meaning of the emotions and how they may affect the negotiation process. The following three steps will help you deal with your opponent's emotions:

1. Listen for reasons. Start off listening to people without seeking solutions for overcoming emotions. Take one step at a time for now and just listen actively. Look at the world through your opponent's eyes to help you understand.

See if you identify any of the following emotions in your opponent:

Fear: We experience fear when we perceive a threat to our physical or emotional well-being.

Anxiety: We become anxious when we fear potential problems.

Insecurity: People feel insecure when they doubt their abilities to function or cope as expected.

Frustration: We become frustrated when something blocks us from reaching our goals.

Anger: Anger usually emerges when people feel threatened.

Annoyance: Annoyance is a lesser form of anger that occurs when we feel offended.

These are only some of the many emotions people may feel during their negotiations. Once you've identified the emotions, ask the person why he or she feels a certain way. Say something like: **"You sound like you may have other thoughts on the issue. Tell me about them."** When you appropriately ask a person to expound upon her feelings, you also continue the rapport-building process.

2. Measure the emotions. Emotions are subjective expressions of the importance that people place on issues. The level of importance may determine the level of the emotion. You can understand the emotion best if you first determine what your opponent finds most important and why. You'll need to do a little investigating. Ask questions like: **"How important to you is this issue?"**

The importance of issues is subjective. What seems important to one person might seem trivial to another. Their reactions will differ. Instead of reacting to an outburst, you should measure the emotion by putting it into perspective. One person might scream and yell if a negotiation becomes frustrating. Another person might get up and storm out of the room. A third person could mask the frustration by attempting humor.

People overreact to problems once in a while. Sometimes outbursts of anger to seemingly minor issues arise from an accumulation of problems. Some people might not deal with problems when they first happen, allowing their anger to build up over time. Eventually, something triggers a reaction, and the person blows up.

In measuring emotions, ask yourself a few key questions: **"How would I react if I were in that person's shoes?" "What might be the reasons the person behaved that way?" "How am I contributing to the negative emotions?"**

3. Evaluate the intensity. Negative emotions can result from a variety of psychological causes such as attitudes and expectations, comfort levels, feelings about the other party, or negative perceptions. Each reason may cause a different intensity level.

Sometimes emotions are so intense that reaching an agreement is not likely. You're better off simply ending the negotiation rather than trying to talk your opponent out of being emotional. Other times the emotional person just needs time to cool down. In those cases you can slowly move forward. Make comments such as: **"I'm sorry that discussing this upset you."** or **"The last thing I wanted to do was upset you."**

Abraham Lincoln's indulgence of his wife's notorious bad temper probably saved his marriage. A story about Mrs. Lincoln's temper was detailed in *A Book of Anecdotes* by Daniel George. It describes how on one occasion Mrs. Lincoln barged into a room where Lincoln and his lawyer were engaged in conversation. She accused her husband of neglecting and insulting her because he had been too busy to run an errand for her. She then left the room and slammed the door. Lincoln turned to his lawyer and said, "That little eruption does so much good for her. It relieves her frustrations. And if you know her like I do, you would be glad she had an opportunity to explode once in a while."

Test Deadlines

During your research to understand the challenge, you should test your opponent's deadline. Deadlines introduce time pressure into the deal. Scheduled events provide an excellent example of a deadline. To illustrate: Greg heads the marketing department of a nonprofit group raising money for cancer research. Five days before the scheduled fund-raising event, Greg learns that the musical band has canceled. Greg now faces the task of contacting a music promoter and finding a replacement band.

"When do you need the band to perform?" asks the promoter.

"Well," Greg explains, "I'm in a rush. How about this coming Sunday?"

"One of my most talented bands is playing nearby on Saturday. They could be there Sunday around noon."

"Great, we'll take 'em," Greg says. "Is their fee similar to the first band's?"

"Oh, no," replies the promoter. "On such short notice the charge will be at least twenty percent more for the day."

The promoter probably could have charged Greg the same amount of money. But she used Greg's time pressure to give herself negotiating power. How could Greg have defended against that power? First, he could have acted indifferent about the need for a band. He might have given the promoter the impression that he really didn't need the entertainment for the fund-raiser, but if the price were fair he would agree to hire the band. That would have eliminated the perception of time pressure.

Break Things Down into Meaningful Units

When our negotiations involve money, we should be leery of people who speak only in terms of percentages. Percentages are good for betting on horses or figuring your chances of contracting a disease. But they often mislead people in negotiations. Breaking percentages down to dollars makes sense. For example, a 25-percent discount sounds like a great deal on almost anything. But if you're buying a seven-dollar pair of socks, 25 percent is pocket change. Even though a 25-percent discount sounds great, its benefit is relative to the price.

Sometimes real numbers might be more than the percentage implies. Take the case of a magazine selling advertising. The magazine boasts that it's the fastest growing because it had a 25-percent increase in sales. But its circulation was only ten thousand people, so the circulation grew by twenty-five hundred. Another magazine, with a circulation of one hundred thousand, grew only 10 percent. But its circulation, in real numbers, grew by ten thousand. The real numbers paint a clearer picture.

Percentages are illusions in many cases. People often use illusions to sway their opponent's perceptions of the deal. Why do you think gambling casinos use chips instead of actual currency? It's easier to slide colorful chips over to the dealer when you lose than it is to peel off hundred-dollar bills. Chips change people's perceptions of money. Intentionally or not, people may use deceptive symbols like percentages in their negotiations to cloud your understanding of the challenge.

Another method of deception that you need to be aware of is "averages." Sometimes we are confronted with averages on such things as the time it takes to complete a task or the average amount of money saved when purchasing a particular product. Keep in mind that an average doesn't always translate into the best deal for you. An average is just an average, and negotiation is the necessary adjustment in the free marketplace.

In addition, look out for people who break the cost of something down to the day. Have you ever seen television commercials offering a product for only one dollar per day? Those "one dollars" can add up to a bad deal if you're not careful.

Test the Opposing Camp

A person's camp is a group of his or her support people: family members, friends, coworkers, managers, professional advisers, etc. One way to get to the bottom of the challenge is to test your opponent's camp. That means asking questions of camp members. If you learn what's going on in their world, you can usually learn what's going through your opponent's mind as well.

I once used this strategy in a negotiation with three men who were business partners. They were selling a parcel of land, but I noticed that one of the partners moved more slowly in making concessions.

During several meetings the partner often seemed preoccupied with other thoughts. He appeared less interested in making a deal. Curious about the partner's behavior, I contacted a friend of his, a businessman with whom I had dealt in the past. At our casual lunch meeting, I brought up the partner's name in general conversation. His friend, cautious not to reveal too much information, explained that the partner was under severe pressure to pay the IRS back taxes. I later concluded that the partner was stalling, trying to structure a payment plan with the IRS before the sale closed so the proceeds of the sale wouldn't go directly to the IRS.

That partner behaved with "conflicting signals." His behavior conflicted with the intention of selling the land. Realizing the partner's dilemma, we agreed to cut the deal as soon as possible, but close the deal at a later date that was suitable for everyone involved.

 Recognize conflicting signals among the opposing camp members, and devise a strategy that appeals to all members of the camp.

See It in Ink

Research on the topic of memory proves that we remember and understand concepts better when we see them in writing or can visualize them in our minds. If you have the time, write down the challenge when you think you have a solid understanding of it. When you see it and read it over, you will understand it even more. You'll also want to write down your goal in the negotiation and the strategy you'll use to overcome the challenge. The more you see the goal in writing, the more likely you are to keep it in mind during the actual negotiation.

Take the time to write down
the challenge and your goals.

Setting the Right Goal

The great American inventor Thomas Edison had a dilemma. He didn't really know what price to ask the Gold & Stock Telegraph company for his stock ticker invention, a device later used by stock brokerage companies. Edison figured that the time and effort he had put into the invention were worth between three thousand and five thousand dollars. But he didn't feel comfortable asking for that much money. So, when the president of Gold & Stock, General Lefferts, came to negotiate with Edison, he asked how much he wanted. Edison was so uncomfortable with the thought of asking for so much money that he found himself speechless. He just stood there, unable to get the words out. Lefferts waited impatiently for Edison's response. Still, the inventor couldn't name his price.

Finally, Edison managed to say, "Make me an offer."

Lefferts responded, "We'll offer you forty thousand dollars."

Obviously, Edison had set his goal too low. How do you know when your goals are too high or too low? What's realistic? Goal-setting takes research. You should know the real value—and your opponent's perception of the value—before making or accepting a price. Once you know the value, you should set your goals realistically high as a seller, and realistically low as a buyer. Research shows that sellers who aim for a high price and buyers who aim low usually end up getting the best prices in their negotiations. However, avoid outrageous or insulting requests. That could make you look self-indulgent and discourage your opponent from continuing the negotiation.

Your goals can relate to aspects of the negotiation other than dollar amounts. An employee might be seeking the goals of better work hours and more vacation time along with a raise. The employee should not base his goals on some arbitrary want or need. He should know what other employees in his position customarily receive in terms of work hours, vacation time, and pay raises. Aiming a few notches higher than what's customary is good goal-setting, but the employee had better have good reasons to ask for more than what others have been given.

Remember to prioritize your goals while realizing that a 100-percent success rate is ideal but not always likely. When you set goals, you should have a clear understanding of which goals are most crucial and which ones you can use as concessions if necessary.

People's emotions often play a role in goal setting. Be aware that strong emotions can sometimes convince you to seek unrealistic goals. Let the facts, not your ego, set the goals.

Setting Limits

What are your limits in negotiation? They are the points, specific to each individual scenario, at which you are willing to walk away from the negotiation. Your limits also establish what concessions you're willing to make in hopes of achieving the desired result. How do you know where to set your limits? It all comes back to research and knowledge. If you know the value of a particular Rolex wristwatch, for example, you'll also know the maximum you're willing to pay for it. Another example is if you're having trouble reaching an agreement with a friend, you know at what point you should stop the conversation before an argument ensues. Sometimes we make the best deals for ourselves by walking away from an unfair deal that exceeds our limits.

Know when you'll need to
stop negotiating and walk away.

In the heat of a negotiation you may not think as clearly. So set your limits ahead of time! This enables you to make fast decisions during the negotiation. Knowing your limits also gives you confidence. You'll know that you're prepared to walk away without hesitation. Ending a negotiation is not failure if you've saved yourself from being cheated. So set your limits and move on to Chapter Six, *Step 3: Introduce New Alternatives*.

Summary

- ⏱ **Contemplate the big picture of a negotiation.**

- ⏱ **Seek a deeper understanding of the challenge by exploring underlying issues.**

- ⏱ **It's dangerous to think your assumptions are the facts.**

- ⏱ **Listen actively—so your opponents know they've been heard.**

- ⏱ **Instead of expressing your disagreement, simply let your opponent know you understand his or her point of view.**

- ⏱ **Present your point of view gently and carefully so your opponent has time to become comfortable with it.**

- ⏱ **Keep an open mind. Realize that the challenge can change from time to time.**

- ⏱ **Recognize conflicting signals among the opposing camp members, and devise a strategy that appeals to all members of the camp.**

- ⏱ **Take the time to write down the challenge and your goals.**

- ⏱ **Know when you'll need to stop negotiating and walk away.**

CHAPTER SIX

Step 3:
Introduce New Alternatives

The Right Alternative

For the first hour of a scheduled five-hour flight, passengers found themselves annoyed and frustrated. Their antagonist came in the form of a four-
year-old boy who preferred running up and down the aisles, screaming and
yelling, to watching the in-flight movie. Even his parents couldn't stop the
rambunctious kid from grabbing other passengers' pillows and blankets. Several disturbed adults tried scolding the boy, but his cries were louder than
his playful yells.

Finally, one of the passengers, a professionally dressed woman who had
remained silent before, called the boy over and whispered into his ear.
Then, standing and holding the boy's hand, the woman escorted the boy to
an empty seat at the front of the airplane. She explained to the boy that he
was now going to help the pilots fly the plane.

A flight attendant, after speaking with the woman, sat down next to the
boy and explained that his job was to look out the window and keep an eye
out for birds flying nearby. That way the plane wouldn't hit any birds. For
the remainder of the flight, the boy kept busy with his new job and left the
other passengers alone.

When the plane landed, several passengers asked the woman how she
came up with such a good idea to keep the child from being "such a problem." She responded, "There were two problems, yours and his. Unfortunately, you were only interested in solving your problem. I focused on
solving the boy's."

The message of that story emphasizes the value of "Step 3: Introduce New
Alternatives." The woman conceived an alternative that didn't have to leave
either the passengers or the boy a winner or loser. In fact, it allowed every-

one to enjoy the flight a little more. The alternatives in your negotiations should offer the same type of benefits.

Invest time in building a negotiation strategy with new alternatives.

The New Face of Negotiation

Before professional baseball was transformed into a gold mine for gifted athletes, players endured with few alternatives in their salary negotiations. One year, in the early 1950s, the management of the Cleveland Indians reportedly mailed contracts to team members for their signatures. Several weeks later, the team's general manager was said to have received an unsigned contract from one of his players. The general manager then sent a telegram that reportedly said, "In your haste to accept the terms, you forgot to sign the contract." A telegram from the player arrived the next day. It read, "In your haste to give me a raise, you wrote in the wrong dollar amount."

Either that player had found a job he loved more than baseball or he had simply reacted to feeling pressured into accepting terms he didn't like. People who feel pressured in their negotiations often become defensive, and their negotiations usually focus on which side wins and which loses. Even if a negotiation ends with an agreement, the feeling of being pressured can convince someone to later renege on the agreement.

The INSTANT NEGOTIATOR system rejects any notion that negotiators should pressure other people into accepting their demands or that negotiations should end with winners and losers. Instead, the INSTANT NEGOTIATOR system offers "Step 3: Introduce New Alternatives," a vital component of the system's win/win negotiating style. Introducing new alternatives focuses on collaborative bargaining. Instead of pitting your strengths against your opponent's strengths, you conceive options that add value to the bargaining for all the people involved, stimulating your opponent's resolve to reach a satisfying agreement.

The concept of introducing new alternatives addresses all that's wrong with common but ineffective bargaining techniques: forced concessions, compromises, splitting the difference, win/lose philosophies, take-it-or-leave-it demands, and us-versus-them approaches. These negotiating strategies, and many more, support the theory that negotiations consist of only two options—win or lose. By introducing new alternatives you provide additional options so both sides can win. With new alternatives people make choices rather than making sacrifices and compromises.

A superior negotiating tool—introducing new alternatives—invites creative, inventive solutions. It suggests that you explore solutions outside of the obvious, in which people can work together, offering ideas and making suggestions. It promotes brainstorming among opponents, and it leads to more satisfying agreements.

Expanding the Pie

In 1994 Mexico struggled with a severe economic recession. In the wake of the recession, one of the country's largest banks, Grupo Financiero Serfin, reportedly faced numerous loan defaults and began negotiation efforts to recoup as much money as possible from its debtors. A May 1999 *Harvard Business Review* report explained how Serfin used creative alternatives to negotiate its way out of potentially huge losses.

Serfin executives created a companywide negotiation framework, standardizing its negotiators' priorities and goals and eliminating their concession-oriented style of deal-making.

In one case Serfin was dealing with a manufacturing company, a long-standing customer of Serfin, that defaulted on a loan. Serfin negotiators reportedly worked with management in securing a third-party investor to take an equity partnership in the manufacturing company, strengthening its financial position and helping it to thrive. Serfin could have taken the manufacturer to court and fought for a settlement on the loan. Instead Serfin executives came up with a creative alternative that added value to the manufacturing company and sealed the banking relationship for future business.

Alternatives such as this can transform a negotiation from a battle of wits into a reciprocal, problem-solving project. Opponents can focus on the components of the deal rather than worrying about whether the other side is out to beat them down.

This step requires imaginative thinking and brainstorming. But don't mistake it for an arduous task. If you've followed the first two INSTANT NEGOTIATOR steps, the information you have about your opponent will help stimulate your thinking process. When you come up with alternatives, list them (in your mind or on paper if you have time) and evaluate the benefit of adding each one to what already exists on the bargaining table. This process is informally known as "expanding the pie," because the pie metaphor helps explain the concept in simple terms. Consider the following explanation:

Let's say you're negotiating with someone over an apple pie. You're both hungry and neither of you is satisfied with splitting the pie in half—you both want three-quarters of the pie. As it stands, the negotiation can only end unsuccessfully because one or both of you would leave dissatisfied. It's now necessary to expand the scope of the negotiation by adding value to it. What if you topped the pie with whipped cream? Then sprinkled it with chocolate shavings? How about vanilla ice cream to go with the pie?

Can you see how the negotiation will take on a whole new life? Maybe your opponent would be willing to take less apple pie if you could give her most of the ice cream, whipped cream, and chocolate shavings. Instead of compromising for half the pie, you would end up with three-quarters of the pie—what you wanted in the first place—and maybe end up with some ice cream as a bonus. Instead of just splitting the pie as it exists, you expand it first, adding value to it. Everyone leaves satisfied. Get the picture?

 Expand the pie by adding
value to the negotiation

Don't take "introducing new alternatives" lightly—it might prove to be the most important step in the majority of your negotiations. (Keep in mind that this step could take minutes, days, or weeks to accomplish, depending on the type of negotiation.) It certainly was an important step for the St. Paul, Minnesota Police Department. Officers there reportedly made repeated attempts to talk a man down from the top of a bridge one day. Despondent about an impending divorce, the thirty-year-old man wanted to jump and kill himself.

Police officers took several approaches in hopes of coaxing the man down. They first tried to create a "friendlier environment" for the man. They removed police cars from view and blocked traffic on the bridge, and evacuated surrounding streets to cut down on noise. Police also called the man's estranged wife to the scene, and even the department's psychiatrist offered his input.

At one point officers learned that the man took an interest in mounted patrols. So they reportedly brought horses to the scene. Nothing was working until one ingenious officer, acting on a gut feeling, offered the man a cigarette. As the man reached for it, the officer grabbed him by the wrist and pulled him to safety. Not only did the police negotiators choose the right alternative, they also used a flexible negotiating style. They started out "tender" by making the atmosphere more pleasant for the man, but the police chose a "tough" alternative by grabbing the man after he had made the negotiation difficult.

Why bother with alternatives instead of fighting emphatically for what you want? The answer is simple. Satisfaction! Remember—successful negotiators satisfy. When people work together to create solutions, the whole psychology of the negotiation changes. The tension that normally accompanies negotiations usually subsides, and cooperation flourishes. Their focus changes from what each person wants individually to how they can get more out of the deal by working together. This approach can help preserve relationships, especially among people who negotiate often, such as business associates, colleagues, friends, and family members.

In the first two steps we talked about empathy—how you emotionally identify with people. In this step you really put that empathy to work. Remember—negotiating is about more than money and needs. It's about people: their feelings and beliefs.

It's crucial that you assess your level of empathy for your opponent. Do you like the person? Do you understand how the person feels? Can you put yourself in his or her shoes? Your insight into other people can help you create alternatives that they are more likely to accept. Without empathy you might create self-serving alternatives.

Former U.S. Secretary of Defense Robert McNamara realized too late the power of empathy. McNamara has written about how he and other American policy makers, along with the leaders of North Vietnam, might have stopped the Vietnam War sooner had they empathized with one another. He writes in *Argument Without End*, "We clearly lacked the understanding of Vietnamese history and culture that would have prevented us from believing that they would reverse course as a function of being 'punished' by U.S. power." McNamara goes on to say that the U.S. bombing of North Vietnam was the Johnson administration's attempt to bargain with its enemy. But the North Vietnamese saw the bombing differently: as an ultimatum.

Create alternatives with a sense of empathy for your opponent.

Now, let's take a look at some examples of how we can use our creativity to introduce new alternatives. (The most effective way for us to provide examples of alternatives is to show them in the text of an ongoing negotiation. However, keep in mind that during this step you are not yet presenting the alternatives. You are simply introducing them into your negotiation strategy. You'll present them later in "Step 5: Go for Agreement.")

A husband and wife have different opinions on how to spend their day off together.

Carole wants to spend the day shopping at a discount mall. Rich wants to go to the beach. How can the couple negotiate an agreement?

Alternative 1. They could do neither. Instead, Carole and Rich could each make suggestions on something else that they would both enjoy together: a movie, brunch at a restaurant, or a drive in the country.

Alternative 2. The couple could go to the beach during the day, go out to dinner at a restaurant near the discount mall, then go shopping in the evening.

Alternative 3. Carole and Rich could go their separate ways for the day doing what each wants, and then spend the evening together doing something of mutual interest.

A car buyer is trying to lease or buy a new car under market value.

Bruce has found the car he wants, with all the options he needs. But he and Joanne, the car dealer, are in a stalemate over the price. What can they do to continue moving toward an agreement?

Alternative 1. Either Bruce or Joanne could suggest throwing in additional options at no additional cost, such as tinted windows and a CD player. Bruce might be willing to pay the dealer's asking price for the car with the extras. And the dealer's cost for the options might be minimal and worth throwing in if Bruce buys the car.

Alternative 2. Bruce could suggest a higher trade-in value for his current car. And if he's leasing, he could request a higher limit of allowable miles per year. That means the dealer will allow him to drive twelve thousand miles per year as opposed to ten thousand miles on the lease. Joanne could offer upgraded tires, an extended warranty at no charge, plus the first two oil changes and car washes for free. But she would hold firm on the trade-in value and the new car price.

Alternative 3. If Bruce is leasing the car, he could also request a higher residual value for the car at the end of the lease. If buying, Bruce could accept the last price offered but make it contingent on financing with a below-market finance rate. Joanne could offer Bruce a demo car—the same model car but with more options—that was used by the sales manager and has a few thousand miles on it. With the demo she could throw in a CD player.

A linen salesman is negotiating an order with a hotel manager.

The hotel manager likes the salesman and wants to do business with him, but a competitor has offered the same linen products at a lower cost. What alternatives does the salesman have? He could:

Alternative 1. Offer the hotel manager a discount if the hotel prepays instead of paying after the products are delivered. This would save the linen company out-of-pocket costs for the wholesale purchase of the product and allow the company to still see a profit.

Alternative 2. Offer to sell the hotel a larger quantity of the product up front and to deliver the product over time as needed.

Alternative 3. Suggest that the hotel purchase a large volume of other products and take a smaller profit margin in hopes of making up the difference in volume sales.

Alternative 4. Think globally by offering to service all of the hotels in the chain at a discount.

Alternative 5. Barter for something of value in addition to cash, such as complimentary hotel or conference rooms.

In each of these examples, you can see how the alternatives relate to the issue at hand. Not only are they practical suggestions, but they also hold enough value for the opponents to feel comfortable considering them and to make easy decisions.

Create Workable Alternatives

Be prepared to face rejection when you eventually offer your alternatives. Some people may have a hard time accepting new ideas, especially when their main focus is only to narrow the gap between the obvious differences. Some negotiators may consider new alternatives unnecessary, or they may think alternatives will confuse the process.

Don't react emotionally to a rejection of your offer. It usually represents disagreement, not disapproval of you personally.

One way to avoid rejection is to think of realistic, workable alternatives in the first place. Your alternatives should not include off-the-wall ideas. They should relate directly to the wants and needs of the people negotiating.

Consider the case of the attorney purchasing tile flooring for her office. She makes an offer below the listed price for tile and installation. But, with her price offer, she includes two bottles of rare, expensive wine that have appreciated in value since she purchased them. The attorney has learned that the tile installer, like herself, is a wine collector. She appeals to the tile installer's passion for wine, convincing him to accept the offer.

In this example, the attorney makes her opponent's decision an easy one by providing an alternative that the tile installer finds value in. The alternative gives him a reason to accept the low offer. And since the tile installer is passionate about wine collecting, the alternative also poses no risk of confusing the negotiation. Were he unschooled in the subject of wines, he might become puzzled or uncertain of the attorney's sincerity.

 Avoid rejection by offering workable alternatives that have your opponent's interests in mind.

Advances in technology are changing the way we live and work. It's inevitable that we must search for new answers and create alternatives that coincide with the changing times. The proliferation of Internet web sites can help with this process. They offer an abundance of information right at our collective fingertips. The more information you have about the issues you're negotiating, the more likely you are to develop valuable, workable alternatives.

Exploring Creative Ideas

In "Step 2: Understand the Challenge," we talked about thinking "outside of the box," that is, developing ideas out of the norm. When you're thinking about new alternatives, I encourage you to think "outside of the box," not with wild ideas, but with alternatives that go beyond the scope of what appears customary or standard.

 Think "outside of the box."

I found success in this way of thinking while negotiating an employment agreement with a promising young salesman. I wanted to hire the salesman at my commercial real estate firm, but he couldn't pay his mounting bills while waiting months for real estate commissions to start coming in. (Commercial real estate salespeople usually work for commissions only—not for salaries.) But I worked out a creative solution.

I decided to pay the salesman a small salary with a below-average commission rate. The salesman was able to pay his bills and break into the real estate business. My company was able to secure a hardworking salesman for a lower-than-average commission split, even after factoring in his salary. That wasn't the standard way of doing business, but it paid off. That salesman eventually became one of the top producers in the company.

Oxford University Professor Edward De Bono has written several books on creative thinking. In *The Use of Lateral Thinking,* De Bono tells a story of a mischievous old and ugly money lender who took a unique approach in trying to win the young woman he wanted. Many years ago the woman's father was a town merchant who owed the lender a huge sum of money. The lender proposed a bargain. He told the merchant and the daughter that he would drop two pebbles, one black, one white, in an empty bag. The daughter would blindly pick one of them. If she picked the black pebble, she would have to marry the lender and the father's debt would be forgiven. If she picked the white pebble, she would stay with her father and the debt would still be canceled. And if the young woman refused to pick a pebble, her father would be thrown in jail and she would starve. They agreed.

Standing in a road surfaced with pebbles, the lender knelt down and insidiously grabbed two black pebbles and quickly tossed them in the bag. The observant young woman saw what he had done, but chose to keep quiet. Then the dishonest lender asked her to choose. Eager to help her father and to avoid marrying the lender, the daughter reached her hand in the bag and pulled out a pebble. But in a split second, before anyone could see it, she intentionally fumbled the pebble and it fell to the ground, and it became indistinguishable among the millions of other pebbles in the road.

The pebble remaining in the bag obviously was black. The lender certainly didn't want to admit he had cheated, so they all concluded that the daughter must have picked the white pebble. She was free to go home, and the debt was forgiven.

The young woman cleverly thought "outside of the box." Most people, after seeing the two black pebbles, would have stopped the deal and accused the lender of cheating. Instead, the young woman used the lender's dishonesty to help her own interests.

Thinking "outside of the box" suggests that we avoid looking head on for solutions to problems. It promotes a more imaginative approach, breaking the problem down into smaller parts and finding solutions for each subpart. I tried this approach one evening while ordering dinner at a restaurant.

The menu offered meatball subs with mozzarella cheese. I asked the waitress to substitute provolone cheese for the mozzarella.

"We can't make meatball subs with provolone cheese," responded the waitress.

"Why not?" I asked.

"Because we make them with mozzarella."

Right then I knew I wasn't working with a creative thinker, so I posed an alternative. "I see that you have ham and provolone sandwiches," I said, breaking the problem down to the ingredients of the sub. "Can you take the provolone you use for those sandwiches and put that on my meatball sub?"

"No," responded the waitress.

"Why not?" I asked.

"Because I wouldn't know what price to charge you," said the confused waitress.

I wasn't desperately hungry at the time, so I figured I'd have a little fun. I asked the waitress the cost breakdown of both the meatball sub and ham sandwiches with no cheese. I knew the prices with the cheese. I then calculated the cost of the cheeses and from there derived a price she could charge me.

"Is that an acceptable price for me to pay?" I asked.

Once again the answer was "No!"

And once again I asked, "Why not?"

"Because we'll have to use more provolone in order to cover all the meatballs, and I wouldn't know what to charge," she replied.

Frustrated over the waitress's apparent inability to imagine anything other than the obvious, I bit my bottom lip and calmly asked, "So how's your pizza here?"

I had obviously chosen the wrong person to negotiate with that night. But at least I got another story out of it. Most of the time, however, thinking "outside of the box" and breaking things down into smaller units will generate workable alternatives that you never even thought possible.They are ways of negotiating solutions to problems instead of negotiating the problems themselves.

If you don't consider yourself a person who typically has creative ideas, you can follow a process for producing ideas. Creative thinking is more than waiting for inspiration. It's a process of gathering as much information about the issue as possible, and then making numerous combinations of the different pieces of the information. Here's an example:

Let's say you're negotiating over the purchase of a living room furniture package. First you would make a written list of all the items included: two lamps, a couch and love seat, two end tables, and a coffee table. You'd want to know the price of each item as part of the package and separately. You'd also want to compare the quality, service, delivery charges, finance charges, and warranties with those of another store.

Then list other items you would like to have but are not included in the package price: a reclining chair, a painting, a floral centerpiece, two large silk plants, a throw rug, and two designer picture frames. Once again, compare prices, quality, etc.

Now that you have a list of all the items, begin making different combinations of them. What if you didn't need the lamps and substituted them with the silk plants? How about omitting the love seat and taking the reclining chair and the throw rug instead? You would want to use the different options also to adjust the price and terms of the package to meet your budget. Rather than accepting the package the way it exists, you would be designing numerous combinations to create a package that would meet your own specific needs.

Designing combinations of information may require a great deal of thought and consideration. You'll want to look at your combinations from different angles, weighing pros and cons. Once you've designed a combination that you think works, you have in essence produced a creative idea. Before you fully implement the idea, have someone you trust scrutinize it to see if it makes sense.

Objective Sources and Neutral Locations

Despite our sincere intentions of finding workable alternatives, we cannot escape the dilemma that our own interests will conflict with others'. Roommates argue over who gets the room with the view. Business partners quibble over whether to take monthly salaries or quarterly bonuses. A landlord wants two months' rent and a security deposit up front, while the tenant is willing to pay just one month and security. One way to overcome conflicting interests is by using "objective sources" as alternatives.

Objective people or things help move people past their firm negotiating positions. Let me explain:

In the case of the roommates arguing over who gets the room with a view, a flip of a coin should do the trick. It's objective and fair because both roommates have the same opportunity for winning. The business partners might seek an answer from an accountant on whether to take monthly salaries or quarterly bonuses. The landlord and tenant might seek the opinion of a real estate attorney to determine the amount tenants customarily pay up front in that market.

In determining the value of a product, for example, you can consult an objective third party, such as a jeweler, to appraise a gold necklace. You can use research materials such as a blue book in determining the value of a car or a consumer magazine that rates the quality of a particular product. Spouses might seek the advice of a marriage counselor; coworkers might seek solutions with the help of a manager. In essence, the goal of objective sources as alternatives is to draw conclusions from standards and principles instead of from arbitrary negotiating positions.

Sometimes a change in surroundings or atmosphere can change the outcome of a negotiation. Certain formal settings, especially your own turf, may present an intimidating or negative atmosphere for your opponents. They may associate the surroundings themselves—walls, pictures, furniture—with an adversarial position or with the inability to reach an agreement if the negotiation is dragging on.

Changing the physical location of the negotiation, such as meeting over lunch or taking a walk in pleasant surroundings, could create a friendlier and more open environment. If you're not making headway, changing the seating arrangements within the same location sometimes can help give the impression of progress. Some of the most effective negotiators I've dealt with avoided sitting across a table from people. Instead, they sit next to their opponents on a couch or in separate reclining chairs.

Although it might not sound logical, new surroundings can spark a new demeanor in people, creating a perspective that the negotiation is moving forward in a positive way.

Brainstorming

The more alternatives you list the better. In fact, even if you have alternatives you know you'll never use, keep them on your list anyway. Sometimes, when you present ideas, they can help the brainstorming process by sparking more suitable ideas.

Most likely, you will brainstorm alone when introducing alternatives to your strategy. However, sometimes it makes sense to brainstorm with your opponent. As I mentioned earlier, this approach may change the psychology of the negotiation, offering a climate of teamwork and cooperation.

When you offer a variety of alternatives, you demonstrate that you're dealing in good faith, with the other side's interests in mind. However, I have one major caution: Don't offer so many alternatives at one time that you end up confusing either your opponent or yourself. Our brains can only process so much new information before we begin losing track. Present your alternatives at an appropriate pace for your opponent, one at a time, and make sure your opponent clearly understands each one.

Brainstorming with your opponent acts as an icebreaker. It may reveal your opponent's most ardent feelings about the negotiation. Ideas you present as brainstorms may seem less threatening than if you presented them in the actual negotiation. The brainstorming session allows you to present ideas in a friendly way rather than as a formal offer or counteroffer. It may also allow your opponent to buy into your ideas. They'll invest emotionally into the idea-producing process, which keeps them in the deal.

When brainstorming with your opponent, be careful not to reveal your strategy.

When brainstorming with your opponent, float a "trial balloon" such as the "what if" question. Your goal is to test your opponent's viewpoint: **"What if we go to the beach today and then we'll shop for your new shoes at the mall tonight?" "What if the company gives me a smaller raise but grants me more vacation time?" "What if we offered you a settlement but asked you to accept a promise of confidentiality?"**

 Test your opponent's perspective with "what if" questions.

"What if" questions serve several purposes:

- "What if" questions give the impression that you're asking for your opponent's opinion. This demonstrates your concern for the other side's interests.

- "What if" questions subtly ask the other side to buy into your ideas. Instead of demanding that they accept your alternatives, you're asking that they simply consider them.

- "What if" questions yield feedback from the other side. The feedback will tell you if the alternative is viable or if your opponent will most likely reject it. You'll want to contemplate the feedback and structure additional alternatives based on what you've learned from it.

I remember a simple "what if" question that I used when I was a teenager. Attempting to reduce my chances of being rejected, I would try "what if" on girls. I would ask, "What if a guy like me asked a girl like you to go out on a date—what would you say?"

If the girl answered, "I would say yes," then I knew I could ask her for a date without being shot down. If the girl replied, "I would say no," then I could eliminate any thoughts of asking her out.

It's also good practice in brainstorming to ask people directly how they arrive at their viewpoints: **"How did you determine the value of the furniture?" "What makes you feel that you've been treated unfairly?" "Why do you think your commission should be higher than that of other salespeople?"**

These types of questions, when posed in a non-cynical manner, encourage further brainstorming. The answers may widen your perspective of the negotiation and advance the process of conceiving more alternatives.

You should come to the negotiation prepared with as many alternatives as possible. List the alternatives ahead of time on a piece of paper. That'll lessen the need for "thinking on your feet" negotiating. You don't want that kind of pressure.

Win/Win Is the Goal—But Not Always Possible

There's a true story about a small, isolated tribe of people that never developed a system of numbers in their native language. They could count to only two. Their entire system was one, two, and the rest was "many." In this language if you had three children, you had "many." And if you had ten children, you still had "many."

The language of the tribe was such that they never thought of counting above two, even though there are an infinite number of things to count. This limited language exemplifies how too many people, especially Americans, are limited in their negotiations by assuming only two solutions exist—the solution that's best for you and the one that's best for your opponent. Successful negotiators don't think that way. Instead they explore a variety of winning solutions for both sides. Numerous alternatives mean more possibilities for win/win negotiations.

We hear a lot about the win/win theory of negotiating. It's a popular message of sales trainers and managers, and rightly so. We should all strive for win/win. But let's also be realistic. Sometimes win/win is not possible.

Inflexible thinking, large egos, and irrational emotions often block the potential for win/win solutions. Introducing new alternatives is the best strategy for dealing with difficult opponents. But when opponents are manipulative or dishonest and trying to win at your expense, it is sometimes necessary for you to move from a tender to a tough negotiating style. You no longer need to worry about their interests in such cases. You must protect yourself from difficult people trying to cheat you.

What if you're on the winning side of win/lose? I believe that if you make a sincere effort to offer your opponent beneficial alternatives and negotiate with the other side's interests in mind, you deserve to win no matter what.

It's not the best result if your opponent feels as though he has lost. But as long as we negotiate with empathy and offer valuable alternatives, we deserve what we get out of our negotiations.

Although we should always strive for win/win, it's not always possible.

Many times you will recognize ahead of time when win/win is likely, especially when you're dealing with negotiators who are flexible in their thinking and who actually enjoy seeking ways to overcome a challenge or solve a problem. When people offer workable alternatives, they reduce their burden to persuade the other side because the alternatives themselves help persuade.

Alternatives and Risk

When you introduce new alternatives, you may also introduce a new element of risk. You'll need to examine the risk closely by comparing the potential benefits of the reward to the downside of the risk. To illustrate:

A salary negotiation between a bond saleswoman and her company management reached an impasse after three days of negotiating. The saleswoman, a top producer in the firm, wanted a larger commission structure plus stock options in the company. Management didn't normally give stock options to employees and found the saleswoman's commission request unreasonable.

Finally, the saleswoman posed a creative but risky alternative. First, she suggested that the company eliminate her base salary. Then she set tiered benchmarks for her production and commissions. The starting commission level was well below her current average. But at every benchmark in production that she reached, the commission would increase sharply. At the highest benchmark, a level that no salesperson in the firm had ever reached, she would then earn stock options.

The saleswoman's alternatives carried inherent risk. If she were unable to produce at a level high enough to earn stock, she would have forfeited her salary for no benefit.

Risk also comes inherently if you're brainstorming with your opponent. You could possibly furnish your opponent with ammunition to help his strategy. Be careful not to cross that fine line between your desire to add value for your opponent and giving away too much information about your negotiation strategy.

 Understand the risks involved in your alternatives.

No Appeasing

Franklin D. Roosevelt once said, "No man can tame a tiger into a kitten by stroking it." He was right! Alternatives are not meant to appease. Some people might initially consider introducing alternatives a tender way to avoid tough negotiating or to appease the other side. They may have a natural tendency to disregard options that might help their opponents.

If you believe that introducing alternatives seems like a tender way to negotiate, don't be fooled. This negotiating style is not only the mark of a successful negotiator, it also characterizes the tough negotiator in a tender negotiator's clothing.

Negotiators who see value in this creative process are smart and driven to get what they want. But instead of turning the negotiation into a confrontational battle, or surrendering to compromise, they shrewdly design an ingenious strategy to win—and to make their opponents feel they've won as well.

John F. Kennedy wrote about the dangers of negotiators who appease. He believed appeasement was an extreme—the opposite of violence, but offering the same detrimental result. Take a moment and read Kennedy's opinion on extreme thinking in negotiations:

"On the one hand are those who urge upon us what I regard to be the pathway of surrender: appeasing our enemies, compromising our commitments, purchasing peace at any price . . . If their view had prevailed, the world of free choice would be smaller today.

"On the other hand are those who urge upon us what I regard to be the pathway of war: equating negotiations with appeasement and substituting rigidity for firmness . . . Neither side admits that its path will lead to disaster— but neither can tell us how or where to draw the line once we descend the slippery slopes of appeasement or constant attack."

In essence, little difference lies in the results of appeasement and hostility. Both threaten your chances of a successful negotiation.

Prioritizing Alternatives

Emotions play a role in how you may prioritize the alternatives. You may be partial to a particular idea because it satisfies you emotionally. New alternatives that add little or no value for your opponent and appeal only to you are basically useless. Once again, keep emotions out of it. Obviously, your alternatives should benefit your negotiation strategy. The tricky part is prioritizing the alternatives based on your opponent's point of view without sacrificing your own needs.

Prioritize new alternatives based on your opponent's point of view.

As you prepare to move to the next step of the negotiation, you should have brainstormed, thought creatively, and introduced new alternatives into your negotiation strategy. You should have also prioritized those new alternatives. Before you move on to the next step, here's an entertaining negotiation that includes creative alternatives offered by actor Jack Nicholson playing the role of Bobby Dupea in the movie *Five Easy Pieces*.

The scene has Bobby bantering with an inflexible waitress while trying to order breakfast at a diner. After his unsuccessful attempts to order the breakfast he wants (which isn't on the menu), Bobby engages the waitress in a clever negotiation. Here's how the scene goes:

First, Bobby asks for a plain omelet and a side order of wheat toast. But the waitress tells Bobby, without apology, that they don't have side orders of toast.

At this point Bobby is skeptical, and he questions the diner's unwillingness to serve a side order of toast. He points out that the diner has bread to make sandwiches and a toaster in the kitchen. So, why no toast? The annoyed waitress suggests that if Bobby wants to talk with the manager, he could, and that she doesn't make the rules; to which Bobby replies:

"OK. I'll make it as easy for you as I can. I'd like an omelet, plain . . . and a chicken salad sandwich on wheat toast, no mayonnaise, no butter, no lettuce. Now all you have to do is hold the chicken, bring me the toast, give me a check for the chicken salad sandwich, and you haven't broken any rules!"

I wouldn't recommend Bobby's caustic demeanor. He didn't win over the waitress as an ally. However, he certainly presented a clever alternative.

Summary

- ⏱ **Invest time in building a negotiation strategy with new alternatives.**
- ⏱ **Expand the pie by adding value to the negotiation.**
- ⏱ **Create alternatives with a sense of empathy for your opponent.**
- ⏱ **Avoid rejection by offering workable alternatives that have your opponent's interests in mind.**
- ⏱ **Think "outside of the box."**

- ⏱ **When brainstorming with your opponent, be careful not to reveal your strategy.**

- ⏱ **Test your opponent's perspective with "what if" questions.**

- ⏱ **Although you should always strive for win/win, it's not always possible.**

- ⏱ **Understand the risks involved in your alternatives.**

- ⏱ **Prioritize new alternatives based on your opponent's point of view.**

CHAPTER SEVEN

Step 4:
Set the Rules

The Equalizer

You've probably heard some married people say, "The reason for our successful marriage is that we never go to sleep angry with one another." People who take this approach are "setting the rules" in their marital negotiations. Here's what they could have said to set the rules: **"If we happen to have different viewpoints over this issue, we must promise to put them behind us and go to sleep happy with one another when we've finished our conversation."** This is an example of how we must "set the rules" in all of our negotiations.

Up to this point you have been focusing on preparing to deal with your opponent. Now, in this step, "Set the Rules," you set the stage for the upcoming negotiation. The rules you set are a prelude to the deal-making process. Frankly, setting the rules sometimes requires a little nerve on your part. The rules you set, often in the form of defining statements that you make to your opponent, suggest that you're fixing the limitations of the negotiation. In fact, you're attempting to control the negotiation process. But your goal is to set the rules without any implication that you are not striving for fairness.

You'll find that you set the rules most effectively if you've sufficiently built rapport and your opponent trusts your motives. When you set the rules, you create more power for yourself than you could ever imagine. It's amazing how few people use this important step.

Rarely are negotiating opponents evenly matched. No matter who's involved, someone typically has the upper hand. The highway patrolman has power over the nervous motorist. The wealthy landlord has power over the financially struggling tenant. Sometimes that powerful landlord might end up being the nervous motorist. The highway patrolman could also be the financially struggling tenant.

Since we face so many negotiations day in and day out, we eventually face some of our deals from a weak position. Setting the rules is especially helpful in these underdog situations. It helps us level the playing field and gain some control over our negotiations. If you believe you already have the upper hand in the negotiation, setting the rules can keep you from losing the control you have.

 Help overcome your lack of power by setting the rules before entering into the actual negotiation.

I urge you to learn this step thoroughly. Practice setting the rules in mock negotiations. You'll be amazed at how much power it gives you. Here's how:

1. Setting the rules adjusts your opponent's expectation level. Consider a banker and a customer negotiating over refinancing a mortgage. The customer wants the lowest interest rate; the banker is offering a rate higher than the borrower expected. The banker could justify the rate and set the customer's expectations by saying, "Before we look at your options, we first must recognize that your lack of good credit places your loan application in a high-interest rate category."

2. Setting the rules creates a perceived power that you don't already have. Here's an example: A husband and wife are negotiating over his plans to attend a football game and her wish that he attend a party at her parents' house. The wife knows that her husband will not concede going to the game because he paid a high price for the ticket several months in advance. The party was planned at the last minute. Despite her lack of power in the negotiation, the wife sets the rules by saying: "I'm happy that you can spend time with your friends at the game. I know how important that is to you. I just hope

you realize how important it is to me that you attend my parents' party when the game is over."

3. Setting the rules transfers power from your opponent to you. Let's say you're negotiating with a video production company, and you know very little about the video production industry. You could transfer your opponent's power this way: "As you probably have realized, I know less about your industry than you do. So, any terms we tentatively agree to today would be contingent upon approval by my intellectual property attorney." Now, your opponent can no longer use your lack of knowledge as an advantage.

How do you know what rules to set? INSTANT NEGOTIATOR offers five general types of rules for you to build on: **Guidelines**, **Boundaries, Methods, Procedures,** and **Behavior.**

Once again, setting rules gives you tremendous power to control the negotiation process. In the following description of each type of rule you'll see statements, in bold, that serve as examples of what you might say to set the rules.

Guidelines

Guidelines draw a blueprint of a negotiation. They initially establish who will attend the negotiation. Haggling as a buyer, you might establish the guidelines by saying: **"I cannot discuss the cost of your services until my wife (or husband) arrives and we review the proposal together,"** or **"Let's have all the partners meet over breakfast and each bring two solutions for this problem."**

Be careful about inviting nonessential people to participate in the bargaining. Any person who has little to add to the dialogue or has no power to make decisions is one person too many. Nonessential participants could muddy the waters and cause you to lose control of the negotiation. Salespeople know this. Family members or friends who don't fully understand the issue can influence your opponent to reject a good deal.

Guidelines also come in the form of dates and times the negotiations will take place, as well as the surroundings or environment of the negotiation. Will you negotiate in the morning or evening, at your home or office, over lunch in a restaurant or sitting on a park bench? Will the negotiation take a formal tone, or is a casual atmosphere more suitable? The time and location can affect the attitudes of the people involved.

 Establish guidelines that draw a blueprint for the negotiation.

Your opponent might feel uncomfortable negotiating in your office, but he may loosen up and negotiate more freely over lunch or dinner. You might feel more comfortable dealing on your own turf, or maybe you negotiate more effectively in less formal surroundings—over cocktails or taking a walk in the park.

The best negotiating locations typically are devoid of interruptions or distractions. It seems logical that you and your opponent should share undivided attention. But I once saw a television news program that explained how some business people take their clients to adult nightclubs to negotiate deals. The haggling takes place amid loud music and clouds of tobacco smoke. I personally think it's valueless to try making deals in adult nightclubs. I certainly don't advocate or practice it. But the news reporter interviewed people who believed the atmosphere helped them negotiate agreements.

That brings up a valuable point. Different people feel comfortable in different surroundings. Take the time to explore what environment will be most suitable for reaching an agreement.

Seating arrangements may seem inconsequential, but don't overlook them. How and where you and your opponent are seated makes a difference. By sitting casually next to your opponent instead of across a large conference table, you could reduce tension in the air. Or you might want to convey the perception of power by sitting behind your desk.

Change the atmosphere or the surroundings of the negotiation if you think
it will help make the people involved feel
more comfortable.

Guidelines also relate to time limits. The proper time limits place pressure on your opponent and prevent people from stalling the negotiation intentionally to hurt your position.

Here's an example of setting a time limit: **"If we cannot reach an
agreement by five o'clock today, I may have to do business with
your competitor."**

Time limits can also work in your favor by taking the pressure off you. In
cases where you believe your opponent is looking for a quick decision from
you, establish a suitable time limit up front. You'll feel less pressure, and your
opponent will have to change his or her time frame.

Time limits preclude wasting time with insincere opponents. If an opponent has little motivation to reach an agreement, you could see no payoff
for the time invested in the negotiation. A real estate agent might set a time
limit this way: "The buyer wants to preview your home this weekend. So
if you're sincerely interested in listing your house with our real estate company, you might want to let me know by tomorrow."

Set time limits that allow you to
negotiate without feeling pressured.

Unlike adults who follow daily schedules, children have few time deadlines. They don't have to be at work or be on time for an appointment. This
gives children extraordinary negotiating power.

Boundaries
Without boundaries, negotiations can run astray, following multiple direc-
tions and confusing the entire process. You can prevent this by saying:

"Let's agree to focus on the issue at hand. If there are other issues, we'll discuss them at the next meeting." I've seen negotiators run so far off track that they eventually forgot their initial reason for the negotiation.

Negotiations can run way off track if you don't set boundaries ahead of time.

This kind of communication breakdown can happen among feuding neighbors. One person resents that his neighbor's dog uses his yard as a bathroom. So the neighbor begins negotiating to find a solution to this problem. In time their emotions get the best of both neighbors, and they dig up more problems: "Your son plays his music too loud, and I don't complain about that," responds the dog owner. "Well, it's not only your dog, but that old car in the side yard is an eyesore in the neighborhood," argues the neighbor. The dog owner retorts, "Speaking of an eyesore, your lawn is full of weeds and looks like a jungle."

You can prevent aimless bickering by setting the boundaries up front. It keeps the negotiation on the right track, focusing directly on the issue at hand.

Boundaries may come in the form of a written agenda that outlines the process. People tend to follow steps precisely if they're written on a piece of paper. It gives them a sense of organization and may prevent them from straying.

Boundaries can help preserve relationships among family and friends. When we establish up front that the negotiation must end with the relationship intact, we send a message that the relationship is more important than the negotiation. Family members and friends can agree to disagree with one another without becoming defensive.

A sense of equity comes to negotiations with the use of boundaries, especially if you have an obvious weakness. By airing your weakness up front, you establish a recognizable confidence. For example, if an attorney with no experience in patent law is head-to-head with an expert patent lawyer, he might air his weakness by saying: **"We all understand that you are the expert in this field, and my experience is limited. But here is how we should direct our meeting today…"** This type of comment helps level the playing field.

Boundaries are also useful for sending a message to the other side that you are informed and knowledgeable. A business owner might say to a wholesaler: **"I want your rock bottom price so I can compare it with your competitor's."** In this case the boundary reveals your power and how far you're willing to go in the negotiation to get the best deal. Your opponent will know you have options, and it diminishes your opponent's power.

Boundaries work as geographic rules too. I once heard these boundaries stated: **"If we cannot reach an agreement ourselves, we would want a court in Florida to settle the case, since the dispute took place in Florida."** Another example is: **"I'm willing to make a serious offer to purchase the truck, but you'll need to drive it to my office for me to inspect."** Geographic boundaries can keep the negotiation on your turf, giving you more control.

Sergeant Joe Friday of the 1960s television show *Dragnet* used to ask for "just the facts, ma'am." He was setting boundaries. You can do this in your dealings, limiting the type of information you want to discuss. I've heard many a story in which a person deviated from the facts to make a point—like the story of the two fishermen. They were trading fish stories, of course.

The first fisherman explained his great catch. "I was standing on the rocks, and I felt an incredible tug on my line. It about pulled me into the water. I fought that sucker for what seemed like an hour. I thought it was a whale but it was only a bluefish. I pulled him in only after my hands began bleeding from all the fighting. He weighed one hundred thirty-five pounds. That's an amazing bluefish."

Not to be outdone, the second fisherman replied, "I was fishing from my boat one day when I suddenly felt my line snag. I could see to the bottom, and the line was stuck on an old pirate ship. I managed to get that line free, and when I reeled it in, hooked on the end was an old ship's lantern. What amazed me, though, was that the candle was still lit."

Before he could go any further, the first fisherman interrupted. "Look, I'll take a hundred pounds off my bluefish if you blow out that candle!"

Everyone's got a fish story to tell. If you don't want to hear it, you can set the rules by limiting your negotiations to only the facts when necessary.

Methods

Methods are the standards that people can rely on to help move them toward an agreement: **"If we cannot agree on a sales price, then let's use the average of four comparable sales to determine the value."**

Too often, negotiators form their positions around some ambiguous principle. How many times have you said or heard, "Well, it's the principle of the matter." People who negotiate with an ambiguous principle really have no standards that guide their true positions. They rely instead on the strength of their resolve to help them make demands. A seller could say: "I won't sell for anything less than..." Have you ever heard someone say that? What if you replied: "How did you come to determine the value?" A typical answer is: "That's just what I feel it's worth!" A negotiation that includes a battle of ambiguous principles usually creates emotional friction and frequently ends with little satisfaction for either side.

 Redirect your opponent's ambiguous principles by referring to methods or standards as a guide.

You can avoid or overcome ambiguous principles by using a method or standard as a guide. You could suggest the use of a professional appraiser who can offer an objective opinion of value: **"I'm willing to make a deal...but it's only fair that we have a professional appraiser determine the real market value."** A mortgage broker negotiating over interest rates may use a standard by referring to Internet sources indicating the national average of interest rates. The goal is to use objective sources that provide factual information and a sense of fairness.

 Consider using objective sources
that provide factual information and
facilitate fairness.

Precedents also serve as "methods." Judges make decisions in court based on what other judges have ruled in the past—precedents they've set. Our daily negotiations can rely on precedents as well. Many companies create policies based on precedents. For instance, salespeople from the same company often solicit the same customers. This familiar conflict requires that someone decide which salesperson wins the customer and earns the commission.

Some companies may require their salespeople to work together with the customer and split the commission. Another policy may require a management official to review the situation and determine which salesperson was the procuring cause of the sale. Usually the solution lies in the precedents set earlier, in a similar conflict.

Using "methods" this way limits uncertainty on the part of the negotiators. Factual information, standards, and precedents are usually objective. These rules especially come in handy as a defense tactic when your opponent is seeking an unfair solution.

Procedures

A once loving husband and wife found themselves embroiled in a nasty divorce and arguing over the custody and visitation of their children. For months neither they nor their lawyers could find a solution. So the couple decided to consult with a priest for the right answer.

After only a few minutes of listening to the problem, the priest offered his suggestion. "You, as the father, should flip a coin in the air," explained the priest. "And you, the mother, should call heads or tails." Then he explained that whoever won the toss would make up two sets of custody rules, one for each parent.

The husband immediately spoke up in disagreement. "That's no solution to our problem. We're right back where we began."

"But no," replied the priest. "Whoever wins the toss makes up the custody rules, but the other goes first in choosing which rules he or she prefers."

This story includes three examples of how procedures can serve as rules in negotiations. The couple used an objective procedure in their negotiation by relying on advice from a respected third party—the priest. The priest himself suggested the objective procedures of flipping a coin and of having one parent make the rules and the other choose first.

 Allow objective procedures to bring an inherent fairness to the negotiation.

Relying on an objective third person helps keep ambiguous principles out of the negotiation. A third person can bring inherent fairness to the process of reaching an agreement. The third person can also facilitate constructive conversation and brainstorming. A negotiator could set this rule by saying: **"Each side will give a ten-minute overview to the arbitrator, who will then make a decision."**

Procedures such as flipping a coin are also objective and inherently fair. A coin flip ends with a winner and a loser. Granted, that might not be the best result. But the inherent fairness in the coin toss gives both sides an equal chance to win. And in cases where one person divides and the other chooses, like the husband and wife in our story, both sides find themselves compelled to offer a fair solution.

Sometimes procedures are policies established far in advance. In my company, I set a policy that required any person who came to me with a grievance to also have two possible solutions to the problem. Before any problem-solving began, the employee knew that I would give fair consideration to his or her opinions on a possible solution.

In a perfect world, both sides would hope to reach a sense of fairness by using objective sources. But it's not a perfect world, as pointed out by Canadian author Lawrence J. Peter, who was quoted as saying, "There are some men who, in a 50-50 proposition, insist on getting the hyphen too."

Behavior

Sometimes negotiators set rules with negative behavior, counting on threats, manipulation, and sheer stubbornness for a shot at victory. This type of tough style can spread a negative tone throughout a negotiation. Those threats, spoken even through a smile, are still negative. Here's one way a negotiator would prevent it: **"The only way this can work is if we agree to get over our emotions quickly and move on to the next issue."**

Our goal is to stop negative behavior in its tracks, but not with the use of more threats of our own. The best way to stop it is by setting negotiating rules such as: **"We both want what's best for both of us. So, let's agree up front to 'lay down our weapons' and talk about how we can find a fair solution."**

Stop negative behavior before it begins by setting behavior expectations for yourself and your opponents.

By setting behavior expectations up front, you put the other side on notice that you want the negotiation to have a cordial tone, and that you don't plan on making threats. This could defuse any defensiveness on the part of your opponent and possibly alter his or her attitude.

I once witnessed a very good negotiator set the rules this way in a land deal. A gas station owner wanted to buy a vacant lot next door so he could expand. The vacant lot was between the gas station and an office building, and the owner of the building also owned the lot.

During the negotiation the gas station owner began playing hardball with the owner. He made some condescending remarks and idle threats, hoping to put pressure on the owner. In response, the owner set the rules by saying, "Look, at the end of the day, no matter if we close this deal or not, we're still going to be neighbors, so we might as well be neighborly." It was a great example of setting the rules, even after the negotiation had begun.

Especially in America, many people believe the best way to get what they want is to literally fight for it. We commonly argue aloud with one another. We say hurtful things. We speak our minds regardless of how our words cause pain in others. This kind of behavior makes negotiating more difficult than it has to be.

Whether people know it or not, most arguments between people are negotiations gone bad. People are negotiating to solve problems, but they are using negative behavior to win. Ironically, fighting most often achieves more hostility, not satisfaction.

Even those people who win a fight will end up paying a price later on to the enemies they've created. This cycle of poor communication is creating a society addicted to violence. But here's the good news amid the bad: You can begin the habit of eliminating fights in your corner of the world by setting behavior expectations before you begin your negotiations. From now on, before you enter into a discussion that you know has the potential for emotional consequences, let the other people know that you're not interested in threatening them, and that any threats directed toward you will end the negotiation. Use comments such as: **"I've always known you to be fair,"** or **"You've always been willing to talk things through calmly."**

Beware of those people who accept violence as a better alternative than negotiation.

Setting behavior expectations is especially helpful in preserving relationships among people who negotiate frequently, such as family members. Siblings could say to each other: **"No matter what decision we come to, it's important that we put differences aside and keep our relationship as close as it has been in the past."** When we make an effort to set behavioral expectations, we have the potential to maintain the affinity we share with friends and family. At the very least, we limit the power of people who want to remain our enemies.

Abraham Lincoln taught us a lesson about setting the behavior expectations of our opponents. When a constituent complained to him, saying he should destroy the Confederate rebels and not speak kindly of them, Lincoln answered, "What, madam, do I not destroy my enemies when I make them my friends?"

Summary

- ⏱ **Help overcome your lack of power by setting the rules before entering into the actual negotiation.**

- ⏱ **Establish guidelines that draw a blueprint for the negotiation.**

- ⏱ **Change the atmosphere or the surroundings of the negotiation if you think it will help make the people involved feel more comfortable.**

- ⏱ **Set time limits that allow you to negotiate without feeling pressured.**

- ⏱ **Negotiations can run way off track if you don't set boundaries ahead of time.**

- ⏱ **Redirect your opponent's ambiguous principles by referring to methods or standards as a guide.**

- ⏱ **Consider using objective sources that provide factual information and facilitate fairness.**

- ⏱ **Allow objective procedures to bring an inherent fairness to the negotiation.**

- ⏱ **Stop negative behavior before it begins by setting behavior expectations for yourself and your opponents.**

- ⏱ **Beware of those people who accept violence as a better alternative than negotiation.**

CHAPTER EIGHT

Step 5:
Go for Agreement

You're Prepared

Anybody who's ever played sports as a kid has heard every coach's prover-bial rallying cry on the practice fields around America. It goes something like this: "Practice does not make perfect—perfect practice makes per-fect." It's a good philosophy to prepare as well as possible before taking on any challenging task. At some point, though, no matter how perfectly you practice, you must perform—otherwise all the preparation means nothing.

This step—"Go for Agreement"—drives home the message that even-tually you need to, as the Nike shoe company says, "JUST DO IT!" That slogan has reverberated around the world because it says a lot in three words. It offers no excuses why something can't happen. The demand is clear.

I suggest that you take that advice once you've prepared sufficiently during the first four steps. Now's the time to execute your plan. This step shows you how.

Using Your Preparation

The progression through the INSTANT NEGOTIATOR steps is comparable to golfing. Before teeing-up, a golfer first learns the par of the hole, and the distance and location of the green. The golfer also examines the obsta-cles such as sand traps and water. The golfer then plans a strategy, choos-es the appropriate club, and sets up. In the final step the golfer swings and hits the ball.

You would suspect that if the golfer prepared well enough the ball should land in the middle of the fairway or even on the green. But many times the ball hits an obstacle, such as a sand trap. In this case the golfer refers back to the preparation steps, examining the distance and direction to hit the ball, avoiding even more obstacles, planning a strategy to complete the hole, choosing the appropriate club, and finally swinging and hitting the ball again.

Just as in golf, negotiators must refer back to their preparation steps to help them overcome obstacles and execute their strategy successfully. This step—"Go for Agreement"—is like swinging and hitting the golf ball. It's the action that follows the preparation.

Often you'll find that your negotiations get off course. People become frustrated, communication problems emerge, your strategy falls short, and so on. Referring back to some of the previous steps is necessary to overcome these glitches and move back on course.

For example, during an attempt to go for an agreement in the settlement of a lawsuit, one attorney may learn that her client failed to reveal evidence that could be detrimental to their case. The lawyer would have to stop her attempt to seek an agreement and move back to "Step 2: Understand the Challenge." She would take the necessary action to more clearly understand the big picture of the negotiation before moving forward to Step 5.

It's best to use the first four steps in their proper order when preparing your negotiation. But during Step 5, you will use the other steps randomly, as you need them. Step 5 is also a time to mentally review your preparations and make sure you've completed each step thoroughly. Have you spent the necessary time to **know your opponent?** Have you researched the other side and empathized with them personally? Have you separated the person from the issue? Do you clearly **understand the challenge?** Could more obstacles be in your way? Have you **introduced new alternatives** that are workable? Can you think of more alternatives? And did you **set the rules** in a manner that your opponent understands them and is willing to follow them?

A Simple Formula

There once was a billionaire wine baron who suffered from a fatal disease. All of his family had died, and there was no one to inherit his riches and vineyards. So the billionaire decided he would leave his fortune to the wisest person among all the people in his town. The billionaire spent months searching and finally narrowed down the choice to one man, one woman, and a young boy.

As a test for choosing the smartest of the three, the billionaire escorted the three into a huge wine cellar with winding hallways and numerous rooms, and slammed the door behind them. Through a tiny window in the door the billionaire explained that he had equipped the door with a complicated lock and whoever could find a way out of the wine cellar first would inherit his fortune.

The man and woman immediately began scurrying around like mice in a maze seeking a way out. They ran from room to room, searching for secret doorways or windows. The boy, instead, sat down on a crate of wine bottles and seemed to become lost in thought. After a while of watching the man and woman running around looking for the secret exit, the boy stood up and walked to the door through which they had entered. He turned the handle, opened the door, and simply walked out. The door had been unlocked the whole time.

For his common sense and assertiveness, the boy had won a fortune. Would you have had the common sense to simply open the door? We all like to think we would. Think back to experiences in your life when common sense could have prevailed but didn't. Have you made mistakes that had a lasting effect on your life?

Many times we forget common sense solutions because our ego and emotions take control of us and cloud our good judgment. As you enter your negotiations, keep the lesson of the unlocked door in your mind. Remember how common sense—and acting on it—prevailed.

During your attempts to reach an agreement, you could experience a myriad of emotions. Your feelings could be hurt or your ego bruised. You might feel anxiety or apprehension. Maybe you're impatient to get the deal done quickly. Whatever the case, your negative emotions can consume your thought process. Don't let that happen. Stay calm and think about the issue sensibly.

Becoming angry can shut down your rational thinking process. It leaves people vulnerable to saying spiteful, mean things. When you feel negative emotions coming on, take a deep breath and try to relax. Remind yourself that becoming outraged is a choice. It's a human defense against being threatened, and you're not being threatened. You're negotiating.

Act in a positive manner. You might even try finding a private place, like a rest room, and forcing yourself to smile while looking in the mirror. This may sound ridiculous, but our physical actions can change our feelings. So, if you look in the mirror, break open a big smile. You'll feel silly at first, but in a few seconds you'll begin to feel some relief from your anger. It really works!

In some cases your opponent might want to anger you on purpose. He might become belligerent just to manipulate you. A smile can hold real value in these cases. Can you imagine smiling at an opponent who is expecting you to be angry? It's a simple way to transfer power to you.

Remember—common sense should prevail. It'll help you keep your cool under pressure.

Persuasive vs. Persuading

Part of seeking an agreement involves persuading people that the alternatives you've presented are fair. But people don't always like to feel as though they've been coaxed into accepting something. They like to think that they can make up their own minds. The well-known French mathematician Blaise Pascal once said, "We are generally better persuaded by the reasons we discover ourselves than by those given to us by others."

You can take this concept one step further in your negotiations. If the alternatives you introduce are inherently persuasive themselves, your opponent can discover the value in each. Your persuasive action in this step should be to facilitate your opponent's discovery of the best alternatives. Following are six universal principles of persuasion that you can use.

The "Yes" Principle

Just as a smile can make you feel happier, saying "yes" over and over can make you feel positive about something. By asking questions that lead to common sense "yes" answers, you can convince your opponent to feel positive about your offer. Consider this example: A manager in a financial services company is trying to resolve a dispute between two top salespeople. They both solicited the same potential customer, and both want the authority to close the deal and earn the commission. Their mutual contact with the customer was coincidental. Neither has more claim than the other to the customer.

The manager, faced with finding a solution to this problem, first devises a group of "yes" questions. He asks both salespeople, "Do you believe we can help this customer with our services?"

Both salespeople answer, "Yes!"

"Are you each willing to go out of your way to provide the best customer service possible?"

"Yes!" they answer.

"Do you believe our company philosophy that the customer's needs come first?"

Once again they answer, "Yes!"

"Since you both agree that you're mostly interested in helping the customer, then you should also agree to work as a team and provide the best service possible. You would also agree that the percentage of the total commission that you earn will be commensurate with how much time each of you spends on closing the deal. It makes sense, doesn't it?" asks the manager.

Their only answer can be "Yes!"

Reciprocity

When you meet someone for the first time and you hold out your hand, what does the other person typically do? He or she reciprocates by extending a hand as well. Your negotiations can work the same way. Favorable gestures can sometimes obligate your opponent to make concessions.

Human nature induces a sense of obligation among people who've been given something by someone else. People feel a need to reciprocate. If you hold a door open for someone, he may be influenced to open the next door for you. If you compliment an opponent on her achievements, she may feel obligated to recognize your achievements as well. These might seem like trivial points, but it's amazing how few negotiators use reciprocity to their advantage.

They could also lead your opponent to making more concessions. Some people might call it the "You scratch my back, and I'll scratch yours" mentality. Although this method might have a negative connotation in some circles, it doesn't have to. Giving to receive is an honorable way of negotiating as long as it's done ethically and sincerely.

Proof

Have you ever "jumped on the bandwagon"? If you think your answer is no, just answer these questions: Have you ever seen any of the following movies: *Titanic*, *Forrest Gump*, *Rocky*, or *The Godfather*? Have you ever owned a Beanie Baby, a Pet Rock, a Hula Hoop, or a Cabbage Patch doll? Did you ever wear bell-bottom pants or a tie-dyed shirt? Have you danced the latest moves? Has your hair been styled to look like a television or movie star's? Do you root for the sports teams that win most often?

Everyone is probably covered here! Most people participate in things that are popular or in fashion, like the latest clothing styles, blockbuster movies, and various fads. We follow the lead of other people. When we see that everybody is doing it, we jump right in ourselves because we've seen the social proof of its benefits. This principle can apply to your negotiations. You have a better chance of persuading people to accept your alternatives when you explain or show how they've benefited other people.

Authority

People tend to make concessions more often to people who carry an aura of power or authority. This doesn't mean that people usually give in to bossy, aggressive people. We simply have a natural respect for people in prominent positions.

A friend of mine is a well-known television news anchor. People recognize her everywhere she goes in her hometown. Her familiarity offers numerous perks. She rarely waits in long lines at restaurants, and she seems to get better service. People commonly approach her for her opinion on various subjects. They recognize my friend as an authority figure. And, whether it's warranted or not, people treat her in a manner they think is appropriate to her "status."

Maybe you are an authority figure; maybe you're not. Just be aware that the perception of authority could work in your favor, or it could work against you if you are typically intimidated by authority.

Liking and Being Liked

As we've discussed, people have a tendency to say yes to people they like. If you understand this from "Step 1: Know Your Opponent," now you should recognize this behavior as a defense as well. Just because you like someone doesn't mean you should freely compromise what you need. Instead, work harder at conceiving alternatives that you sincerely believe will help people you care for while satisfying your needs as well.

Limited Opportunity

People become more motivated to act when opportunities appear scarce. The economic principle of supply and demand makes this point. People are more motivated to buy when something is in limited supply. Have you ever been in a store where a mob of people crowded around a table in the middle of the aisle, hoping to be the first to grab the discounted merchandise?

In negotiations, people will move toward an agreement faster if they feel they must take advantage of a limited opportunity.

Here's a warning, though! This does not mean that you should offer a limited number of alternatives. The more alternatives you present, the more value you bring to the negotiation. The principle of scarcity comes into play when any one of the alternatives appears so valuable that your opponent feels eager to accept it.

Each of these principles of persuasion will affect your negotiations differently. Sometimes only one or two may apply. Be aware of them as both offensive and defensive measures.

Keeping Your Integrity

Comedian Flip Wilson is said to have cautioned, "Don't let your mouth write a check that your body can't cash." Wilson's way with words made him a success in the entertainment world. The point he makes will help you find success during this step.

You may have already told your opponent that you plan to negotiate with his or her interests in mind. You also may have brainstormed alternatives with your opponent, and you have already set the rules. In essence, your mouth has written the check. Any action you take or anything you say that seems contrary to what you've said in the previous steps may cause the other side to question your integrity.

As you enter the heart of the negotiation, you must have the willingness and ability to follow through with what you negotiate. As Wilson cleverly pointed out, your actions during this step—during the actual negotiation and beyond—must back up your words.

 "Don't let your mouth write a check that your body can't cash."—Flip Wilson

Confidence

Your words and actions must convey a tone of confidence as you present your deal. You want your opponent to know that you are serious about reaching a fair agreement and confident about your ability to do so.

A good negotiator who may not feel self-assured about entering a negotiation will still portray himself as confident. Good negotiators never reveal their uncertainty to their opponents, for fear that they will appear vulnerable. If you do not typically feel certain about your ability to seek an agreement or are unable to mask your lack of self-confidence, you can follow several mental exercises to help.

1. Be prepared. Nothing will give you as much confidence as being completely prepared to deal with an opponent. Knowledge of your opponent, the challenges you face, alternatives you can present, and the rules you've set have all given you power. Recognize that power. Allow yourself to accept it. Think about how you can use that power to negotiate the best agreement possible.

If you don't feel prepared, take the time to refer back to the first four steps. Review your information and move through the steps again with your opponent.

2. Encourage yourself. People are what they think. So think positive thoughts about yourself. Tell yourself that you're confident. Then act confident. Sit or stand up straight. Break open a smile. Lift your head high. Feel proud of all your accomplishments. Focus on your positive traits. And repeat to yourself that you have powerful negotiation skills and you believe in your ability to negotiate fairly.

3. Test your thoughts. Close your eyes and allow your mind to wander for a minute. Then ask yourself if your thoughts were positive or negative thoughts. If they were negative, ask yourself why. Are you trying to discourage yourself? Why would you want to be discouraged? Do you fear making a mistake? Are you angry or frustrated about something? Are you being critical of another person?

These are reasons to lack self-confidence. Get to the bottom of your discouraging thoughts and change them. Think about all the things in life you are thankful for. What makes you happy? What makes you feel powerful? In what circumstances have you felt confident before? Relive that feeling, and keep it with you as you enter your negotiation.

Don't take life so seriously. Enjoy the negotiation process. Concede to the inevitable fact that you will make mistakes once in a while, and consider them learning experiences.

Presenting the Deal

Look and Speak the Part

In the 1960 presidential campaign, Vice President Richard Nixon squared off in a televised debate with Senator John F. Kennedy. The debate was also broadcast on radio. The majority of people who watched the debate on television determined that Kennedy had won the debate over Nixon. The majority of radio listeners, however, felt that Nixon had come off as the more promising candidate. Why the disparity between those people who watched and those who listened?

Kennedy's physical presentation made the difference. He looked healthier and more vibrant. And his nonverbal communication—such as gestures, body language, and facial expressions—told a different story to viewers. Nixon, on the other hand, looked tired. But, although his presentation lacked charisma, Nixon's message was well prepared and his information was easily understood. People who listened to the radio focused more on the content of what each candidate said, because they could not take into account the visual aspects of each candidate's presentation.

What can we learn from this? Presentation matters! During "Step 5: Go for Agreement," you will begin presenting your alternatives to your opponent. You're ready to make the deal. But no matter how good your ideas seem in a negotiation, if you don't communicate them effectively, physically as well as verbally, your alternatives could end up worthless.

 Adapt your presentations by taking into account the need for nonverbal as well as verbal messages.

Verbal Communication

You probably can remember a time when someone tried to explain something to you but you were so distracted you didn't listen. The distraction may have come from an oddness in the person's voice or speech patterns. Maybe the person was using words you didn't understand. Or maybe the person spoke too quickly or too slowly. Whatever the case, the information didn't transfer to your brain. The person failed to communicate the message.

Maybe you've also failed at presenting your ideas clearly. People generally have difficulty getting their messages across. A study of one hundred U.S. companies reportedly found that when supervisors talked with workers, only 20 percent of the message was understood. Even at the highest levels of management, 10 percent or more of the messages were not clearly understood when executives discussed issues.

Some studies suggest that people will forget 90 percent of what they hear after three days if they haven't taken notes or seen visual aids. These shortcomings in human communication routinely form barriers to effective negotiations.

The solution to this problem is to over-communicate. Take a look at the following graphs to understand.

In the perfect world the "sender" communicates the message and the "receiver" understands 100 percent of the message.

In real life, considering people generally understand only a portion of what they hear, the "sender" must over-communicate to get the message across. Don't ever assume an opponent understands your point completely. Expect incomplete communication.

How do you over-communicate? Simply make your point by stating it two or three times in different ways. Then, ask the other person what his or her thoughts are on your comments. Ask the person if you made your point clearly.

Because some people communicate their messages poorly, you, as a "receiver," should over-receive the message in order to understand it as clearly as possible. Use your active listening skills (see Step 2) to help with over-receiving.

Don't ever speak off the cuff when you're going for agreement. If you have the time, practice your presentation. Repeat it over and over again until you are comfortable with it, just as you would if you were preparing for a speech. Be careful, however, not to simply memorize each sentence. You don't want the presentation to seem insincere or "canned."

If you're in the middle of a fast negotiation and you feel compelled to respond quickly—don't if you're not prepared. Pause. Think about what to say. You might even let your opponent know that you're thinking by saying, **"Hmm…let me think about that for a minute."** If you need more time to work out what you want to say, slow down by asking to take a break for a drink of water or to use the rest room.

Stop and think about what you should say in your presentations. Don't try to speak off the cuff.

Choose the appropriate words and stay positive. Language, even when you and your opponent are speaking the same one, can be confusing. In some parts of the United States people call soda "pop." Some people call tennis shoes "sneakers." In the South people say "y'all." In the Ohio Valley they say "yens," and in the Northeast they say "you guys" (even for girls). The English language itself is confusing. People drive on a parkway and park in a driveway. There is no ham in hamburger. A camel's-hair brush is made from squirrel fur. I once asked a clothing store clerk where I could find a pair of dungarees. She later learned I was talking about blue jeans. There's reason to believe that we can easily miscommunicate our ideas by choosing ambiguous or regional terminology.

The goal in choosing the appropriate words is to paint a clear picture for your opponent. You'll want to avoid colloquialisms or phrases that only some people use. Imagine someone in Texas asking to have gravy served atop his spaghetti. Gravy on spaghetti? It's perfectly normal to have gravy on your spaghetti if you're an Italian American from southern New Jersey. Spaghetti sauce is "gravy" to some people.

Use language that your opponent will understand.

Avoid using technical terms or jargon if there's a chance the other person will not understand you. Your opponent could lose track of the conversation and become confused. Simplify your terminology.

If you find yourself talking in technical terms or using jargon, simplify your terminology so it's easier for your opponent to understand.

When we listen to one another, it's natural for us to form an impression in our minds of the person talking. Our past experiences, biases, education, cultural backgrounds, and expectations all factor into how we perceive that person and whether or not we're interested in listening intently to what the person has to say. Because interpretations are so subjective one message may have varying meanings.

Our choice of words in a presentation may seem motivational to one person and ludicrous to another. People listen subjectively. So try using simple, plain English that won't muddle your opponent's listening process.

A person's tone of voice plays a major role in how another person interprets the message. Present your deal using positive words with a pleasant tone of voice. Use common euphemisms for negative words. Here are a few examples:

Instead of "problems" use **"challenges."**

Instead of "give up" use **"concede."**

Instead of "deadline" use **"time frame."**

Instead of "defend" use **"protect."**

Keep in mind that you always want to present your alternatives in a positive manner, and always maintain a perspective of finding value for your opponent in the deal.

Speak clearly and concisely. In many cases, people in the midst of a negotiation are seeking answers, not long, drawn-out explanations. Keep your presentations brief and to the point. However, a brief presentation doesn't necessarily mean you're seeking a brief negotiation. You may want the negotiation to continue in some cases, if it will benefit you.

Each point you make during the negotiation should be direct so the other side doesn't become confused. In some cases you should present the same idea two different ways to help make the point clear. For example: **"We agree to a bonus of one-fifth of the net profit, a total of twenty percent."** The comment includes both the terms "one-fifth" and "twenty percent." It might seem redundant, but it clarifies the point.

Avoid mumbling or speaking in a monotone. People will understand more clearly if your voice inflections are expressive and if they vary in pitch and tone. Studies on human communication suggest that 55 percent of what people understand comes from the other person's tone of voice. You can motivate your opponent with an expressive tone of voice that's appropriate for the circumstances.

When appropriate, yield to your feelings about the issue at hand. Speak with an expressive tone of voice while keeping control of your emotions.

Verbalizing your seriousness and concerns may seem appropriate in some cases. But remember to keep your emotions in check. It's best not to let your opponent know when you are angry.

Avoid using verbal pauses such as "um" or "uh." They make you appear unprepared or nervous. Verbal pauses also can distract your opponent from paying close attention. When you need to pause, simply say nothing—make no sound.

Observe proper etiquette. George Clemenceau, the "Tiger of France," was riding to the Versailles peace conference. His young secretary was griping about all the "diplomatic baloney" she was expecting from the participants. "It's nothing but a lot of hot air," she complained.

"All etiquette is hot air," answered the premier, "but that is what's in our automobile tires, and see how it eases the bumps?"

Psychologist Robert Silver once said, "Etiquette and manners are the social lubricants that prevent people from rubbing each other the wrong way." Remember to include common pleasantries such as: **"please," "thank you," "excuse me for interrupting,"** and **"may I offer a suggestion."** Good manners leave a lasting impression on people. They can endear you to your opponent.

If you ignore the proper etiquette,
your opponent could ignore you.

Avoid bravado. Some negotiators mistake bravado for tough negotiating. They're different concepts. Tough negotiators may act stubborn and drive hard bargains, but bravado is simply talking big even if you have little to offer. People who lack self-confidence sometimes compensate with pomposity. They use comments such as "I wasn't born yesterday," or "I don't get mad, I get even." This behavior can backfire. It may discourage your opponents, disconnecting them mentally from any of their earlier intentions to find a fair solution.

Avoid bravado!

You have little need for arrogance if your negotiation strategy includes workable alternatives and a desire to negotiate with your opponent's interests in mind.

Rely on questions. Inevitably during a negotiation, you will run into trouble and become confused about how to continue. Maybe it'll be an unexpected position that your opponent is taking. Or maybe your opponent rejects all alternatives and starts to play hardball.

The first measure in dealing with confusion is to raise questions. Be candid with your opponent. Ask what he or she hopes to gain out of the negotiation. Use questions to get your opponent talking. And refer back to Steps 1 through 4 to move back on track.

Minor sticking points are inevitable. Overcome them simply by asking more questions.

Try humor. Laughing makes us feel good. Try to interject humor into your negotiations. Even during INSTANT NEGOTIATOR Steps 1 through 4, humor can help you prepare for the final negotiation. It builds rapport and keeps the conversation amicable.

What if you don't consider yourself funny? You don't need to have comedic talent for this. Do some research. Find books on humor or search the Internet. Keep a collection of humorous lines or jokes that you can use in different situations. Find jokes and adapt them to the issues in your negotiation.

It's best to keep the humor pertinent to the subject at hand. Don't be afraid to use self-deprecating humor. It demonstrates humility. People tend to like other people who are humble. Good-natured humor is a good way to defuse a tense situation. It allows you and your opponent to let down your guard a little and relax.

Ethnic jokes or jokes about the opposite sex are **not** appropriate. Do not participate in offensive humor. Period!

Appropriate humor will ease tension and help the negotiation survive trouble spots.

Nonverbal Communication

Pay attention to body language. Some studies on human communication have found that as much as 40 percent of the information we learn from other people comes from nonverbal communication such as body language and appearance. During your negotiations, people will assess you based on your clothing, your hand gestures, your facial expressions (including whether you're smiling or not), the firmness or weakness of your handshake. These factors and many more can reveal much about people's personalities and feelings.

You can find a lot of books about negotiation that teach you how to read body language. Here's the problem: There is no empirical evidence that pinpoints the particular meaning of every type of body movement.

In other words, understanding body language is a guessing game, not an exact science. Trying to guess your opponent's personality or mood by reading only body language is a mistake. You may have heard that a person with arms crossed is sending a message that he or she is annoyed and not willing to be open to suggestions. I don't know about you, but I cross my arms when I'm cold. Body language misinforms as much as it informs. So don't rely on it 100 percent.

People behave with two types of body language: conscious and unconscious. Keep this in mind. Try to be conscious of all your body movements. Be aware of what you're doing. Different people will interpret your body language in different ways. So be conscious of yourself, and act with the intention of emitting confidence. Move with deliberate motions. Smile when you're supposed to. Be calm. Avoid rushing or making odd movements, like tapping your fingers, rocking in your chair, or flailing your arms and hands as if they're uncontrollable. Odd or extreme movements will distract your opponent and make you seem nervous. Exude a cool, calm attitude.

Exude a cool, calm attitude.

Here's an experiment for you to try. Next time you are talking to someone, gaze over her shoulder as if you are looking at something. Chances are the person you are talking to will also turn and look in that direction. You have distracted her by breaking eye contact. She no longer recognizes everything you are saying and is most likely trying to figure out what you're looking at.

Eye contact keeps you and your opponent mentally connected. It sends a message that you want the other person to pay attention. Your opponent will keep that attention longer if you maintain eye contact. People who gaze at the floor or ceiling or avoid eye contact seem insincere, unconcerned with the other person. It can make the other person feel distant and distract them altogether.

Maintain eye contact.

Your mission is to communicate your deal so clearly that your opponent understands exactly what you're saying. Take into consideration how poorly people communicate, and how little they really hear and remember. Take the extra time to evaluate your opponent's understanding of what you've presented. Repeat yourself if necessary, and ask for feedback.

In Your Hands

You've reached a milestone! You now know the INSTANT NEGOTIATOR five-step system. You have laid the foundation for building wealth and happiness by taking the time to learn the most effective negotiating system I've ever seen.

When I negotiate, I keep track of my progression through the steps with my fingers. This may seem elementary, but it works. It's a way of remembering the steps in the proper order and keeping track, especially in a fast-paced negotiation in which you have limited time. With this memory tool, you'll have the steps with you wherever you go.

KNOW YOUR OPPONENT.

 **UNDERSTAND THE CHALLENGE.**

 **INTRODUCE NEW ALTERNATIVES.**

 **SET THE RULES.**

 **GO FOR AGREEMENT.**

What you achieve in life is in direct proportion to how well you negotiate! I've said this before, and I believe it. You should, too. As you begin using the INSTANT NEGOTIATOR steps, you'll see how the effects of each small negotiation are cumulative. Remember, this is a life strategy. The benefits to you accumulate negotiation by negotiation. Over time you can build wealth and create stronger personal and professional relationships.

There is still more to learn about how to use the steps most effectively. Before we move forward with the next part of the book, "21 Strategies with Tactics and Defenses," here's a chance to test your knowledge of the five steps. Read the following negotiation story about a man who's considered one of America's most effective negotiators. See if you can identify the INSTANT NEGOTIATOR five steps.

The Great Communicator

In his book *For the Record,* former presidential chief of staff Donald Regan tells the story of how President Ronald Reagan used his negotiation skills to make great strides in seeking an end to the Cold War.

Ronald Reagan waited impatiently in the doorway of the Villa Fleur d'Eau in Geneva. When a limousine finally pulled into the driveway, the president, ignoring the freezing, blustery winds, shed his overcoat and hat and ran down the steps to the limo. The seventy-four-year-old president smiled and stretched out his hand to greet Mikhail Gorbachev as he emerged from the car. In his typical amiable style, Reagan grabbed the Soviet leader's elbow and assisted the younger man up the villa's front steps. Reagan and Gorbachev had never met before.

Geneva was the setting for negotiations between the two world leaders over military weapons and ways to reduce the risk of nuclear war. Cabinet members and military experts surrounded the two men, positioned to work out the details of any agreements. But President Reagan focused on learning more about his counterpart. He wanted to know Gorbachev not just as the leader of the Soviet Union; he wanted to know what made this man tick.

At a temporary stalemate in the negotiations, Reagan seized an opportunity to get to know Gorbachev personally. He leaned across the table to Gorbachev and said, "Why don't we let our experts figure this out? You and I, let's go for a walk, just the two of us...get some fresh air and see what this thing is all about."

The Soviet leader agreed, and the two men, accompanied only by their interpreters, strolled to a summer house near the mansion's pool. There they sat and talked for almost an hour. When it was time for Gorbachev to call it a day, Reagan walked him to the limousine, with some final small talk, responding to Gorbachev's invitation to host the president one day at the Kremlin. "I'd love to do that," said the president. "But only if you come to America first."

The second day of negotiations found Reagan and Gorbachev sitting in overstuffed lounge chairs drinking Russian tea together. They acted like two old pals just killing time with small talk. When Reagan's chief of staff notified the president that it was time for the meeting to begin, Reagan replied, "Who cares? Mikhail and I are having a good time sitting here talking."

As the negotiations got under way, the friendly tone changed to a more serious one. Reagan expressed his frustration with the Soviets' military presence in Afghanistan and Central America. He implied that their military actions suggested that the Soviet Union wasn't interested in peace. The atmosphere was tense. Each man spoke frankly about his suspicion of the opposing leader. Gorbachev raised his concerns about Reagan's Strategic Defense Initiative, and he raised his voice to express that concern.

Despite the tension, Reagan stayed cool and controlled, and listened intently to Gorbachev's passionate arguments. By paying close attention, Reagan began to understand the Soviet perspective of America and Soviet concerns about its nuclear weapons program.

The Geneva summit ended with several minor agreements relating to airline landing rights and cultural exchanges. But, most importantly, the leaders of the world's two most powerful nations learned that they could talk to each other one on one. They found common ground by telling stories of their pasts. And they agreed to continue talking, to meet in Washington and Moscow, to continue their dialogue about the potential for lasting peace.

What took place in Geneva during that summit was more than a negotiation between diplomatic leaders. It was Ronald Reagan's own personal negotiation with Mikhail Gorbachev. Reagan took steps in his negotiation similar to those you have learned from the INSTANT NEGOTIATOR system. Can you identify any of the steps in this story? Take a moment to test yourself. Read the story again and see if you can identify each step.

Now, see if you guessed the steps correctly:

Step 1: Know your opponent. Reagan graciously met his counterpart with enthusiasm. He took the time to talk with Gorbachev, share stories of their pasts, and drink tea. Reagan was a master at building rapport.

Step 2: Understand the challenge. Reagan knew that negotiations about military weapons wouldn't end after a two-day summit meeting. But he took the time to listen to Gorbachev's concerns, to test his hot buttons, and to see how Gorbachev would react when he raised the issue of Soviet military actions. Although their language barrier was an obvious challenge, Reagan didn't allow it to prevent private conversations with his opponent. Reagan knew he had to find a way to keep both sides talking despite the mistrust between the negotiating teams.

Step 3: Introduce new alternatives. At one point in their conversations, Gorbachev suggested that Reagan should visit Moscow. Reagan said he would but suggested that Gorbachev visit the White House first.

Step 4: Set the rules. Reagan set the rules at one point by asking Gorbachev to leave the formal negotiating table and take a walk with him to the summer house. In doing so, he set guidelines by which he wanted to continue his negotiation.

Step 5: Go for agreement. Reagan and Gorbachev made their presentations and ultimately agreed on several small issues. But most importantly, they agreed to continue their talks in hopes of reducing the number of nuclear weapons in the world.

Well, how did you do? Did you recognize the five steps? It wasn't easy with this type of negotiation. Political negotiations move through the five steps over and over for long periods of time. It could take years to reach agreement on primary issues. But the smaller issues may take only hours or days to agree upon.

That's how all the negotiations in our lives go. Sometimes we negotiate quickly on a specific item or issue. Other times we negotiate over the same issues repeatedly throughout our lives. Now you have the tools to help you deal with any type of negotiation.

There's another reason we chose Ronald Reagan to make a point. During this negotiation he treated Gorbachev like an old friend. He used a tender style of negotiating. However, at other times during his presidency Reagan exhibited a tough negotiating style on occasion, such as the time he called the Soviet Union the "evil empire." In his ongoing negotiations with the Soviet Union, Reagan adapted his style, moving between the tender and tough styles when appropriate. That's the mark of an effective negotiator.

Negotiating Tools

There's still much more to know about how you can use your new nego-tiating skills most effectively. In the next section you'll learn a variety of strategies, with tactics and defenses. You may have heard of, or even used, variations of them in the past. We'll examine the pros and cons of each, and most importantly, ways in which you can defend yourself against opponents who use them against you.

Summary

- As Flip Wilson says, "Don't let your mouth write a check that your body can't cash."

- If you feel unprepared to negotiate, review the first four INSTANT NEGOTIATOR steps to better prepare.

- Look and speak the part when presenting your deal.

- Adapt your presentations by taking into account the need for nonverbal as well as verbal messages.

- Stop and think about what you should say in your presentations. Don't try to speak "off the cuff."

- Use language that your opponent will understand.

- If you find yourself talking in technical terms or using jargon, simplify your terminology so it's easier for your opponent to understand.

- When appropriate, yield to your feelings about the issue at hand. Speak with an expressive tone of voice while keeping control of your emotions.

- If you ignore the proper etiquette, your opponent could ignore you.

- Avoid bravado!

⏱ Minor sticking points are inevitable. Overcome them by simply asking more questions.

⏱ Appropriate humor will ease tension and help the negotiation survive trouble spots.

⏱ Be aware of your body language.

⏱ Exude a cool, calm attitude.

⏱ Maintain eye contact.

⏱ Follow your progression through the INSTANT NEGOTIATOR five steps using your fingers.

CHAPTER NINE

21 Negotiating Strategies with Tactics and Defenses

Strategy 1: The Flinch

Moon O'Brian kept his fingers crossed and his feet scurrying along the snow-covered New York City pavement. Nighttime had settled on this Christmas Eve, and Moon realized that the stores along Fifth Avenue would soon close. He was on a mission, hoping to find a last-minute Christmas gift. Moon had had no luck at three stores. They didn't carry the particular necklace and matching earrings that he had promised to buy for his wife. Moon, so nicknamed because of his large head and omnipresent smile, scrambled along, frantically searching for a store that stocked the gift he needed.

Moon eventually darted into a well-known women's clothing store. Without wasting a second, he accosted a salesman and hollered out his request, with his big smile, of course.

"Sir, do you have this necklace and earring set?" Moon showed the salesman a magazine ad.

"Yes, we do," the delighted salesman answered. "Wait right here and I'll bring them out." Moon felt not only ecstatic but relieved that he wouldn't have to face his wife's disappointment.

The salesman placed the jewelry set on the counter for Moon to survey. "It looks like the same set in the picture," said Moon. "How much are you asking for the jewelry set?"

The salesman replied, "It's nine hundred dollars, plus tax."

Suddenly Moon jerked upright and roared, "What! Nine hundred dollars! Wow!" Then he stood quietly at the counter, shaking his head.

The salesman, noticing Moon's sudden change in demeanor, quickly responded, "What were you expecting to pay?"

"Not that high of a price," Moon said dejectedly.

"Well, since it's Christmas Eve, I know I can get you ten percent off if you're willing to buy it now," the salesman offered.

Moon graciously took his 10-percent discount. With the savings, he treated his wife to dinner at her favorite restaurant, where he presented her with the necklace and earrings she wanted so much.

Moon's best negotiating strategy had worked. He always jerked his body and growled when anybody quoted him a price on anything. He practiced something called the "flinch" negotiating strategy. Moon's goal in using the flinch was to throw the opponent off track and lower his expectation level regarding Moon's motivation to buy. The tactic behind the flinch is to do just that—flinch as if the sound of the price is physically painful to hear. Physical movements are accompanied by expressions like "You're kidding!" or "How much?" or "What!" All of these demonstrate shock and dismay over the high price.

The unfortunate salesman reacted to Moon's strategy and gave in, offering a discount. How could the salesman have defended against the "flinch"? Simple! He could have rationalized the value of purchasing the jewelry at his store, saying: "We offer a lifetime guarantee to fix the necklace if it ever breaks. Plus our service here is unequaled. The price of this jewelry set is only one component of your total purchase…and surely our price represents value when all things are considered."

Reasoning and justification are the best defenses against the flinch. Furthermore, the salesman should have recognized that Moon was running out of time because it was Christmas Eve night. He could have remained silent and waited for Moon to give in.

The flinch is the first of twenty-one common strategies that we're introducing as tools for different negotiating styles. Some of the strategies may fit your style, and you'll love how they work. Others you may find inappropriate. That's why this book does not advocate any of the strategies presented in the following pages; it simply points out some commonly used ones.

But keep in mind that even if you're not going to use a particular strategy, you still need to know how it works so you can defend yourself against it.

Strategy 2: The Budget

Goal: Negotiators use "the budget" to send a message that they want to purchase a product or service but their budget doesn't allow them to pay the price quoted. Governments use this strategy when hiring outside contractors to make bids based on government budgets. The negotiator also hopes that this strategy provokes sympathy for his apparent inability to buy something he wants or needs. The negotiator then leverages that sympathy, convincing the opponent to make concessions.

Tactics: Any of your opponents who use "the budget" might say something nice about your product or service first. That way you have no reason to become defensive. Then the opponent will indicate a desire to buy, but he'll say his budget is limited to a lesser amount: "That's a great-looking stereo system. I'd like to buy it, but I only have six hundred dollars left to spend," or "Our company would like to hire your services, but our annual budget allows for only seventy-five percent of the cost you quoted."

Defense: Realize that most budgets are not set in stone. As a seller, you could suggest to your opponent that you'd work out a payment plan (if it were possible): **"If you don't have enough money right now, I can help you. You can pay half now and make payments over the next six months."** In addition, offer a variety of ways to structure the deal. For example, a salesperson could initially keep costs low by phasing in services over time or by working out volume discount packages.

Strategy 3: Cherry Picking

Goal: This strategy is primarily useful for buyers who are purchasing a variety of items. The goal of the negotiator is to get a quote on a volume discount package, then try to buy only the lowest-priced items in the package.

Tactics: When buyers compare the bids of more than one seller, they may find that the price of some items is higher among the sellers and others are lower. The cherry picker requests a cost breakdown; then he or she buys only the lowest-priced items that each seller has to offer.

For example, let's say you sell restaurant supplies. A buyer comes to you and asks for a package quote on fifty large pots, fifty medium-size pans, and fifty small pots. You quote a price based on the buyer's purchasing all the items from you, and, at the buyer's request, you give him a cost breakdown of each set of pots and pans.

The buyer makes the same request of two other restaurant equipment dealers, then he comes back to you and orders only the fifty small pots— the lowest-priced items, not the package deal. Then the buyer purchases the large pots from another dealer and the pans from yet another, all the while obtaining a package price without buying the whole package. In essence, the buyer "cherry picked" only the lowest-priced items from each dealer.

Defense: Never give out individual prices on package deals. Just give a total price. Hold firm by saying: **"The only way we can deliver this low price is because it's a package price."**

Most buyers prefer to buy a volume of items from one supplier because they spend less time and money on administrative costs. You should understand this when facing a cherry picker. A small concession on the total price of all the items can usually convince a buyer to stay with one seller: **"I can discount the total price only if you agree to purchase the entire package from me."** This kind of statement makes the deal contingent upon the buyer's purchasing all the items, not just the few that have the best comparative prices.

Strategy 4: Deadline Pressure

Goal: We're all used to deadlines. We're forced to meet them every day. We set appointments with clients, prepare proposals for competitive bidding, check in and out of hotels at designated times, and pay our bills by a certain date. In negotiations, people use deadlines to place time pressure on their opponents, forcing them to make decisions within a specific time frame.

Tactics: When someone wants to place a deadline pressure on you, he or she might say as a buyer, "I plan on making a decision by Friday, so if you can't give me a price by tomorrow I'll need to contact your competitor." A seller might say, "This discount offer is only good for one more day; then the price goes up." In personal negotiations, you'll hear things like, "If you don't organize your stuff in the garage by tomorrow I'm going to throw it in the garbage" or "If you don't give me time to complete this project now, I'll be forced to work this weekend and miss your sister's wedding."

Defense: Some deadlines are true, some are false. Questioning the deadline will help you distinguish the difference. If a salesman says a special offer will end, ask: **"Why it is ending?"** or **"If you can give me this price today, why can't you give me the same price tomorrow?"** If the response makes no sense, you'll know it's a false deadline.

Don't give in to time pressures easily. Ask for as much time as you need to make a decision. If your opponent proves the deadline is real, however, you face a decision of either making the best deal possible at that time and living with it or walking away from the deal.

Strategy 5: The Deadlock

Goal: Many negotiators equate deadlocks with failure. They believe that if they reach a deadlock, then they lack the ability to negotiate effectively. But there's really nothing wrong with deadlocks. You need to keep that in mind especially when your opponent doesn't. That's what your opponent wants you to believe, so you'll make a concession and admit "failure."

Tactics: One effective way negotiators implement the deadlock is by simply saying: "It seems that we're deadlocked on this issue" or "Unfortunately, we've reached a deadlock." Skillful negotiators will neither act resentful about the situation nor place blame on you for the deadlock. They're usually matter-of-fact about it, and they wait to hear your plans about how to break it. In some cases, your opponent may cause you to question your strategy and leave you wondering if you should make further concessions.

Defense: Your defense against the deadlock comes in the form of change. Make changes in the deal that creatively add more value for both sides. You can suggest changing the time frame of the negotiation. You can change negotiating team members. You can also think about changing the issues you were hoping to reach agreement on. Sometimes, deciding to agree on only part of the issue and revisiting other parts later works in helping to unlock the deadlock. You might say: **"Since we've both worked so hard at finding a solution, I'd hate to see us walk away with nothing. Why don't we agree on these initial points and meet next week to further discuss the remaining issues?"**

Strategy 6: Escalation and De-escalation

Goal: The "escalation/de-escalation" strategy is useful in a few different ways. First, an opponent can implement an escalating authority strategy against you. This forces you into negotiating over and over with several members of the opposing team at different times. Each team member would have a different level of authority. Because this process becomes mentally and physically exhausting, it could diminish your expectation level and self-confidence. Furthermore, as you move through the tiers of negotiations, you risk revealing more and more information about your strategy and motivations.

"Escalation and de-escalation" can also refer to price. Some negotiators will agree to a price, but when it's time to close the deal, they'll change that price. Is this ethical? Sometimes—depending on the circumstances. I've seen cases in which a landowner reached a tentative agreement on a sales price with a buyer but later received a better offer. The seller then renegotiated with the initial buyer, asking for a price higher than the second offer. This seemed ethical because the seller had a legitimate, higher offer, and the first offer was only tentative.

Tactics: I've seen colleagues become victims of the escalating authority strategy when making deals with large corporations. The corporate executives would assign several people to the negotiation. The first person would have limited authority and reach a tentative agreement. Then my friend would meet with the second corporate negotiator, then a third, and sometimes more. Each negotiation revealed more and more about my friend's negotiating strengths and weaknesses, giving the last corporate negotiator a superior edge.

When it comes to dollar amounts, I've had several de-escalation tactics thrown at me. Once I was at a real estate closing when the buyer's two corporate attorneys presented a check that was a hundred thousand dollars less than the price we had contractually agreed upon. My opponents suggested that they couldn't get the authority from their company to pay the price written on the contract. After much discussion, I called their bluff, stood up, and began walking out the door. Suddenly the attorneys asked me to wait while they left the room to talk privately. When they came back into the room minutes later, they presented a second check—this time with the correct dollar amount. I got the feeling they always took two checks to their closings.

Defense: In this example I called my opponent's bluff. I took that risk because I had a contingency plan if the deal died. I was working with another company that wanted to purchase the same parcel. Calling your opponent's bluff works well in some cases. Another defense is to deal with the potential problem up front. Let your opponent know that you won't stand for any tricky last-minute surprises: **"I plan on seeking a fair solution that we both would be contractually bound to honor."**

If you're involved in a high-ticket negotiation like the real estate deal I was in, ask for a large deposit that your opponent wouldn't want to lose.

Strategy 7: "Oh...it's done already."

Goal: The "Oh...it's done already" strategy is used a lot by attorneys. They file lawsuits first, then begin negotiations. This strategy helps place them in a favorable negotiating position—one that their opponents have little control over.

Negotiators use this strategy to suggest that the work has already been completed, shipments are on the way, ads have gone to print, contracts have already been accepted, checks are in the mail, and so on. It implies that the deal is already in motion, with little chance of changing it.

Tactics: The tactics for this strategy are useful in numerous types of negotiations. For example, a mechanic could repair your car before giving you the final price. He could then defend his price by saying, "I've already incurred the costs of the parts and labor."

Defense: The best method of protecting yourself from this strategy is by establishing control of the deal up front. Ask for an estimate before having any work done. Put your opponents on notice that they should not take any action before reaching a mutual agreement: **"I'd like to compare your price before I agree to have you perform the work."**

Strategy 8: Good Cop, Bad Cop

Goal: Negotiating teams find a lot of value in the "good cop, bad cop" strategy. It's designed to weaken a person's negotiating position by pitting him against two different types of opponents—an aggressive, critical person and a sympathetic, understanding person.

Tactics: Anybody who's ever watched a television show about policemen has seen the "good cop, bad cop" tactic in action. While interrogating a suspect the bad cop berates and threatens him, promising to put the suspect in jail for life. Then the bad cop leaves the room and the good cop comes in to build rapport with the suspect, acting as though they are on the same side and hoping to cajole more information from him.

This is also a classic tactic with salespeople. How many times have you heard, "I would love to accept your offer, but my manager won't agree to anything but full price." In these cases, we don't actually see the bad cop. I've also seen car buyers use this tactic. A wife acts as if she's in love with a car and would do anything to buy it. The husband is uninterested in the car and wants to leave. The salesperson, seeing a deal halfway to closing, makes concessions just to appease the husband.

Defense: This strategy can't work against you if you're negotiating with only one person. Therefore, use "Step 4 : Set the Rules" and offer to negotiate with the person who has complete authority to negotiate a deal.

Associating the two opponents as one negotiating position also serves as an effective defense. You can say to the opponent with the most desirable offer: **"Since you're speaking for both of you, I'll assume your partner agrees with everything you're telling me."** You can also question the opponents' different styles by saying: **"It seems that you and your partner don't want the same thing out of this negotiation. Maybe we should meet again later after you've made up your minds."**

Strategy 9: You Have to Do Better

Goal: Some negotiators call this strategy the "crunch." It works especially well for buyers and sellers. Your opponents could use this strategy to suggest that your offer isn't good enough. It's a non-binding counteroffer that doesn't pin your opponent to a specific dollar amount.

Tactics: Let's say you attend a garage sale and offer twenty-five dollars for a set of lawn chairs. Your opponent can say, "You have to do better than that!" Your opponent has told you not only that she is not interested in selling at that price, but that she has protected her negotiating strategy by not counteroffering with a specific price. Now you're not privy to the seller's price expectations.

This tactic works for buyers, too. Consider this scenario: A banker offers a home buyer an 8-percent fixed-rate mortgage. The buyer says, "I need a better rate than eight percent!"

The banker responds, "Well, what rate did you have in mind?"

"One of the low rates that your competitor is offering," says the buyer. This leaves the ball in the banker's court. He knows the buyer isn't willing to name a rate, so he's forced to make some kind of concession to keep the ball rolling.

Defense: As a seller, you can defend against this strategy by reminding the buyer that the deal includes more than just price. Other factors like service, quality, reliability, and honesty all justify the price or terms. If you're a buyer and the seller says, "You have to do better than that," you can respond with the simple question: "Why?" This throws the ball back in your opponent's court and keeps the discussion moving forward.

Strategy 10: This Is the Final Offer

Goal: When negotiators suggest that they are making a final offer, they also send a message that they are willing to make a commitment and close the deal. With this strategy, your opponents hope that the suggestion of their commitment convinces you to accept the offer. How and when this strategy is used in the negotiation impacts its effectiveness. For instance, posing a final offer at the beginning of the negotiation might have no effect on you because you would have little time and emotional investment in the deal.

Tactics: There are countless ways your opponent could implement the "final offer" tactic. It depends on the type of negotiation taking place. If you're selling something, your opponent could say, "This is my offer. Call me by tomorrow if you accept it." In a personal negotiation an opponent could say, "I'm not interested in spending vacation time skiing. I want to go to a beach. Let me know which beach you would prefer."

Any time that negotiators pose a final offer, they commonly leave opportunity to continue the negotiation. So a final offer doesn't necessarily suggest that the person wants to stop negotiating. For example, the person who preferred the beach to skiing could leave the door open for some other type of vacation.

Defense: As we mentioned, people who use the "final offer" tactic will usually leave openings for further negotiating. Listen for clues to openings such as *probably, unless,* or *if*. These words may suggest that your opponent is not fully committed to ending the negotiation and might be bluffing with the "final" offer.

In some cases, you might want to point out what your opponent has to lose by not considering alternatives, or test your opponent by walking out of the negotiation. By far the best solution is to use "Step 3: Introduce New Alternatives" and conceive as many options as possible to keep your opponent talking.

Strategy 11: Higher Authority

Goal: If you've ever purchased or leased a car from a dealer, then you've had experience with the "higher authority" strategy. A salesperson will typically say that he has to get his manager's approval on any deal you've presented. The salesman's lack of decision-making authority actually gives him power. It gives him a reason to reject your proposal. The "higher authority" strategy places someone else in charge of making the final decision. Consequently, it weakens your position because you have to reveal your offer before renegotiating with the decision-maker.

Tactics: The "higher authority" tactic is most effective at the end of a negotiation, when all the terms have been tentatively agreed upon. A salesman might say, "OK, this deal looks pretty good, but I'll have show it to my manager and get her approval." In some cases, the manager would enter the picture and pick up where the salesman had left off. Other times a higher authority really doesn't exist; it's just an excuse for the salesperson to come back with new demands, reworking the deal to his or her advantage.

Negotiators can use many different types of higher authorities, such as spouses, friends, managers, partners, and boards of directors, just to name a few. Sometimes they really do play a role in the deal; at other times they're excuses to buy time and come back with a counteroffer.

Defense: In the INSTANT NEGOTIATOR five steps, we talk about asking to deal with the decision-maker. It'll help you defend yourself against the higher authority strategy. Ask your opponent up front: **"Do you have the authority to make a final decision on the terms we agree to?"** If the person doesn't have the authority, then ask to speak with someone who does.

You can also defend yourself by referring to "Step 4: Set the Rules," establishing time rules, especially if the opponent is simply stalling. When an opponent defers to a higher authority, let him or her know that you'll need an answer from the higher authority by a specific time.

Another defense is to suggest that you have opportunities to negotiate a better deal with a competitor. You could say: **"I don't want to miss out on the deal offered by your competitor, so I'll need to have your decision right away."**

Strategy 12: The Lowball

Goal: The "lowball" offer kick-starts the negotiation. But, at the same time, an opponent can use it to deflate your expectation level. The lowball works for both sellers and buyers, and in personal deal-making as well.

Tactics: A seller can lure a buyer with lowball advertisements by listing an incredibly low monthly payment in an ad for a house. Interested buyers eventually learn that the low payment is based on the buyer's making a 30-percent down payment and paying three points to buy down the interest rate—unreasonable terms for the average home buyer.

Lowballing buyers make outrageously low price offers with no regard for the real value of things. They sometimes throw in extras, hoping the opponent will find value in them. Extras could include a fast closing or the promise of future business. In personal negotiations, a lowball could relate to responsibilities. For example, in a negotiation between roommates over who does what household chores, one roommate, as a starting point, could make a lowball offer on the number of chores he or she is willing to perform.

Defense: As the seller, you can defend against the lowball by stating the benefits of the products and services that justify your asking price. Explain in detail the reasons your price seems fair.

As a buyer, watch out for sellers who use enticing lowball offers. Ask a lot of questions about the details of the offer. Find out what the catch is in the deal.

In personal negotiations, make strict comparisons between your opponent's offer and what you think is fair. Let your opponents know that you're seeking a fair agreement even if they're not: **"I believe we can reach an agreement if you're willing to be fair and reasonable."**

Strategy 13: The Nibble

Goal: Since many people are impatient negotiators, they often concede on seemingly minor issues just to get the deal done quickly. Nibblers understand this concept. They will ask you to throw in a little bit here and a little bit there to make the deal better and better. In essence, they'll nibble away at you.

Tactics: The nibble is most effective after negotiators have struck a deal. I once hired a one-man company to steam-clean the carpets in my office building. Just as the guy was completing the work, I said to him, "Now, that price you quoted includes cleaning the two Persian throw rugs, right?" I was just asking, but the man answered this way, "Well, not really. But I'll clean them for you anyway." I had used "the nibble" to get the throw rugs cleaned at no additional cost.

Some people are great at this. I've witnessed women asking for a free lipstick after they've purchased a whole makeup kit. I've seen people buying shoes ask to have socks thrown into the deal at no additional cost. Computer hardware dealers might throw in a larger monitor to close a sale. This tactic is extremely effective because people don't want to spend time quibbling over things that seem immaterial. What they don't realize is that nibbles add up to a big bite of savings.

Defense: You can say no to a nibble just as easily as some people can ask for one. The carpet cleaner could have simply said, "No, cleaning the throw rugs will cost you another ten dollars." If you're willing to stand firm long enough, some nibblers will give up and take the deal.

Offering a price list also works as a handy defense in some cases. The list should include a variety of mixes and matches. For example, a computer store could offer the price with or without the larger monitor, making it very clear to the buyer that the upgrade has a higher price. Written prices also add legitimacy. People are less likely to test a price when they see it in writing.

Strategy 14: Competitive Bidding

Goal: The idea behind competitive bidding is to pit competitors against one another as a means of securing better offers.

Tactics: The owner of a telemarketing company is expanding, opening a new office in a different market. She needs quotes on phone systems from suppliers in the market. She invites three different phone system suppliers to meet her at her office—all at the same time. As the suppliers sit together in her waiting room, the owner calls each person into her office, one at a time, to make a bid for the contract. The suppliers know they're in a competition, so they all come to the table with their best prices.

Defense: Effective selling plays a major role in defending against competitive bidding. Sell the benefits that come with your price. Separate yourself from your competitors. Offer unique and creative deal packages that meet the opponent's needs. And gradually propose added-value alternatives instead of making costly concessions.

Strategy 15: Take It or Leave It

Goal: In some cases the "take it or leave it" strategy simply cannot work. Take a hospital emergency room, for example. Imagine saying, "Take it or leave it" to the price you want to pay as medics wheel you in on a gurney.

But "take it or leave it" does work when a person has no incentive to make the deal if he or she must concede any further, or when negotiators have incentive but have exhausted their options and want to test their opponent's resolve. It also applies to relationship negotiations and to negotiations in which conceding further will set a bad precedent for future negotiations.

Tactics: Skillful opponents won't say the words "take it or leave it" for fear they could offend you. Instead, they'll find a less threatening way of saying it: "Unfortunately that's the highest price I can afford to pay" or "I'll have to report you to the department head if you're not willing to comply with company rules." When an opponent presents "take it or leave it," he or she will often back it up with a legitimate reason, hoping you won't perceive it as a bluff or a threat.

Defense: I've seen people completely ignore the "take it or leave it" tactics used against them. They just keep talking about how to make the deal better. This is a powerful defense. It works best when you have a variety of alternatives to add to the deal. Moreover, test your opponent's sincerity: **"I can't accept this offer the way it stands now."** This comment tests to see if the opponent really means "take it or leave it."

You can also confront your opponent. **"If you're not interested in working out a better deal for both of us, then I'll have to contact someone who is."**

Strategy 16: "What If?"

Goal: Negotiators gain power in their deals by extracting as much information as possible from their opponents. That's the idea behind this negotiation strategy. Your answers to your opponent's "what if" questions could reveal more than you want your opponent to know.

Tactics: The owner of a small office building is haggling with a painting contractor over the price of touch-up work. The building owner asks, "What if I purchased the paint and had it delivered to you—how would that affect the price?" The difference in the price could reveal the painter's labor costs and profit margin. The owner would have uncovered information and used it to his advantage.

In another negotiation, Joan, a legal secretary, does not like country music; she prefers jazz. But her office manager, Shirley, comes in early every morning and sets the radio to the country music station. Joan has expressed her dislike for country music, but Shirley won't bend. So Joan asks, "What if we just work with no music on?"

Shirley answers, "I like listening to the radio because the station runs contests and you can win money." Joan has unveiled Shirley's motivation and could always negotiate listening to another station that has similar contests.

Defense: Since you know that "what if" questions are meant to take information from you, answer them with questions of your own. The painter mentioned earlier could have answered the question about the paint this way: "Why are you asking? Can you obtain a discount price on the paint?" By answering with a question, you can counter the "what if" and learn more information that will help your strategy.

Strategy 17: The Phony Problem Solver

Goal: The win/win negotiating philosophy has left the door open for pseudo win/win deal-making. Many people act as if they want to help you solve your problems, but they really want you to lay your cards on the table so they can use the information to their advantage. We call these people "phony problem solvers."

Tactics: This tactic is all about skillful communication. Phony problem solvers build rapport and make their opponents feel like friends. Then they say things like, "Let's talk openly about what we need so we can help each other" or "Tell me what I can do to help you solve this problem."

Defense: You'll be able to recognize "phony problem solvers" because even though they ask you to talk openly, they avoid revealing any of their own cards. The best way to deal with this strategy is to ask open-ended questions of your opponents. Your questions should be probing but sincere. See "Step 2: Understand the Challenge." In addition, be sure to limit the amount of information you volunteer without being standoffish.

Strategy 18: The Decoy

Goal: The "decoy" moves the focus of attention from the most important issues to noncritical issues. It's meant to distract you, leading you to believe the opponent wants something she actually has little interest in. Why is the decoy effective? It limits your knowledge of the negotiation's real challenges.

Tactics: A home buyer makes a low price offer but includes the seller's expensive dining room furniture in the contract. The seller spends so much time and emotional energy fighting to keep her beloved furniture that she places less significance on the low offer.

Defense: Know exactly what you want out of the deal, and don't make concessions on the issues most important to you. Be skeptical of an opponent's interest in side issues. Ask questions about his or her reasons for certain requests: "Why are you requesting dining room furniture? Is there something in particular that you liked about the furniture?"

Strategy 19: Beware of Relationships

Goal: Negotiators commonly use their existing relationships with opponents as reason for the opponents to make concessions.

Tactics: Negotiators implement the "relationships" tactic with simple comments like, "Look, we've been friends for a long time…" or "If you really care about me…" Negotiators will use this strategy for two reasons: Either they believe the issues are more important than the relationship at that particular time, or they believe the relationship is strong enough to overcome the issues. This strategy can give you insight into where you stand with your opponent.

Defense: The "relationships" strategy preys on a person's emotional connection to his or her opponent. Don't let it offend you. Keep your emotions under control. Then take a hard look at the relationship. Ask yourself if it's worth giving up more than you had initially wanted to. Consider the fact that your opponent might be bluffing, and that the relationship is not really threatened. Then look for alternatives that would help you preserve the relationship and satisfy your opponent at the same time.

Strategy 20: Reluctance and Indifference

Goal: The Ecuadorian essayist Juan Montalvo was quoted as saying, "There is nothing harder than the softness of indifference." What a powerful statement! When someone doesn't care if the deal is made or not, the opponent faces an uphill battle.

Tactics: There's an old story about J. P. Morgan and his interest in purchasing a mining tract owned by John D. Rockefeller, Sr., one of the few millionaires in the early 1900s. Because Rockefeller, for some reason, couldn't meet with Morgan, he sent his son John D. Rockefeller, Jr. At the meeting, Morgan started by asking, "Well, how much do you want for the mining tract?"

"Mr. Morgan, I think there must be some mistake," said John D., Jr. "I didn't come here to sell. I understood you wished to buy."

By expressing his indifference about the sale, young Rockefeller limited his opponent's negotiating power. Your opponents could attempt this strategy, too, using a tone of reluctance. For example, when you make an offer, your opponent could respond by saying slowly, "Well...I don't know... I'm not really sure." His apparent reluctance in accepting could entice you to up the offer.

Defense: Look at the motivations of your opponent instead of the issue being negotiated. Use "Step 1: Know Your Opponent" and try to identify what the opponent is feeling and thinking: "You seem reluctant to accept the offer. Can you tell me about your thoughts?" Then use "Step 3: Introduce New Alternatives" to find a way to help the opponent through the decision-making barrier.

Strategy 21: Compromise

Goal: Negotiators use compromise if they have no better alternatives to offer, or if they're not willing to try brainstorming for other options. Compromise is an easy way to avoid negotiating. Requests to compromise sound like fair bargaining, but in reality they require both sides to sacrifice their interests.

Tactics: Negotiators often make requests such as, "Let's split the difference," or "You take half and I'll take half." Any option that doesn't allow you to reach most of your goal in a negotiation is a compromise.

Defense: "Step 3: Introduce New Alternatives" offers the best defense against compromise. By adding options to the deal, rather than dividing what's at stake, you create the chance to satisfy both sides. You can offer comments such as: **"By splitting the difference we both lose. How about this option..."**

Another defense against compromise is to make extraordinarily low or high offers. Let's say you and an opponent are three thousand dollars apart in the purchase of a house, and you know your opponent is going to ask you to "split the difference." You can make a lowball offer. Instead of losing fifteen hundred dollars, you could offer to move five hundred. Your low-

ball offer deflates the opponent's expectation level and moves you closer
to your goal.

Two Universal Defenses

A defense that works wonders against all tactics is humor. Humor makes it
easy for you to negotiate tough on the issues without offending anyone.
You don't have to be a comedian, but you can lightheartedly tell your opponent that you recognize the tactic he or she is using against you: **"OK, I
use the 'flinch' too in my negotiations,"** or **"You're not going to pull
the 'decoy' on me, are you?"** or **"Look, 'take it or leave it' is one of** *my*
best tactics, too."

You should make these comments in a nonaccusatory way, with a smile
on your face. Let your opponent know you're having fun with it. Then follow up the comment with a sincere suggestion to work together in making
a fair deal: **"That's the 'final offer' tactic, isn't it? Look, I believe we can
make a deal here if we work together on this."**

Another powerful defense is silence. You may have heard the quote, "A
closed mouth gathers no foot." After someone uses a tactic against you,
simply remain silent.

When you remain silent, your opponent may begin feeling uncomfortable and begin talking again. That's what you want. The more your opponent talks the more information you can obtain from him. Silence also
implies your indifference or reluctance, convincing your opponent to continue talking to keep the deal moving forward.

Silence also comes in the form of changing the discussion to a different
topic—staying silent on the issue but talking about other things. Once
again, this approach implies that you're indifferent about making the deal,
and it could encourage your opponent to make concessions.

The Most Powerful Defense

At the risk of being redundant, I urge you to study these strategies—not necessarily so you can use them as weapons but so you can learn how to recognize when an opponent uses them against you. At that point you can defend yourself with the suggestions we've made.

Keep in mind that your most powerful defenses against any of these twenty-one strategies and many others are the INSTANT NEGOTIATOR five steps. The steps possess built-in defenses. That's what makes them such powerful negotiating tools. By following the steps thoroughly, you limit the power of any opponent who's using a strategy intended to place you on the losing side of a win/lose negotiation.

CHAPTER TEN

How to Negotiate with the Opposite Sex

Gender Differences and Stereotypes

A father and son are involved in a car crash. Both are critically injured and rushed to the hospital. When the boy is wheeled into the operating room for emergency surgery, the surgeon takes a look at the boy and says, "I can't operate on this boy. He's my son!"

How could this be? His father was in the car.

Have you considered that the surgeon might be a woman…his mother?

Women are surgeons and men are nurses, too! But some people, despite gender diversity in the workforce, still picture in their minds a surgeon as a male and a nurse as a female. Too many people, in their negotiations, still tend to make judgments about others based on stereotypical thinking.

Do men and women always stereotype with malice? Probably not. The fact is that women and men have differences in the way they communicate. Those differences often appear in their conversational styles. Some of the differences are biological; others are the result of socialization. People have developed stereotypes based on some of these common differences. Nonetheless, stereotypical thinking and communication gaps between women and men hurt negotiations. They create false assumptions about the wants and needs of our opponents, and may result in conflicts rather than agreements.

The goal of "How to Negotiate with the Opposite Sex" is not to examine the reasons people stereotype, or to explore the science behind gender differences. It is meant to point out that some women and men you negotiate with may have differences in their conversational styles, and that the differences can often muddle negotiations between people of the opposite sex. The goal here is to understand some of the differences and overcome them by using the INSTANT NEGOTIATOR five-step system.

Believe It or Not

When I set out to write about communication differences between women and men, I realized the potential risk involved. Some people might become offended by the suggestion that women and men take on different conversational styles. But this issue is too important to dance around. If there are real differences, as many researchers suggest, negotiators need to know at least the potential for those differences and how they may affect their negotiations.

This issue is not clear cut. There are fine lines between the differences, and many women and men have no differences at all. Despite all the various opinions on what makes women and men different in the way they communicate, I decided to face this issue head on. I simply took information from research material on female and male behavior, combined it with my negotiation experience, and plugged all of it into the INSTANT NEGOTIATOR five-step system.

One thing I'm most proud of is that the INSTANT NEGOTIATOR five steps, regardless of differences in conversational styles, inherently solve miscommunication among all people. So even if you don't believe that some of the gender differences that I point out in this chapter are real, just follow the five steps as you learned them earlier, and you won't run into any problems.

At the same time, take heed if you don't believe differences exist. You could miss an opportunity to negotiate a better deal for yourself by being unwilling to admit that you may lack an understanding of the opposite sex.

How Nurturing Plays a Role

Sociological studies consistently conclude that most cultures socialize their females and males quite differently. For example, we use pink to identify females and blue to identify males when they're born. The separation of the sexes is so ingrained in our culture that we've not only accepted the practice of using colors to distinguish sexes, we also honor this system as if it were nature's mandate.

As children, boys are often encouraged to compete in aggressive sports or play with toys, such as guns, that relate to hostility and war. Sometimes this could lead grown men to rely on aggressive and competitive behavior in their negotiations. Their behavior typifies what they were essentially "trained" to do as children.

On the other hand, many little girls play house and learn how to comfort their baby dolls. They may focus more on building interpersonal relationships, avoiding competition, and developing a knack for cooperation and collaboration with their peers. When a female learns from an early age that she should be nurturing, those tendencies may become predominant when she attempts to reach agreements.

In countless ways, we create two significantly different cultures for females and males. Sure, men can be nurturing and possess what are perceived as more feminine traits. And women may be aggressive and possess what are perceived as masculine traits. But the very fact that we have categorized certain human traits as "masculine" and "feminine" reinforces the notion that men and women have significant differences that we should not ignore in our negotiations. Neither is more or less appropriate for negotiating effectively. They're simply different.

It's not as important to note that differences between women and men may exist as it is to understand the degree of those differences. Women and men often want the same results out of their negotiations, but the degree to which they want those results may be at opposite ends of the spectrum.

Conversational Styles

Of course miscommunication exists between women and men. In many cases, they have different perspectives of life in general (not to mention all of life's problems and how to deal with them). The differences in their values sometimes dictate the way they communicate. In many cases, a person looks at the other sex from a perspective that has developed from the manner in which he or she was raised. Consequently, each person will negotiate from a different frame of mind.

Each person may perceive the other sex from a perspective that has developed from the manner in which he or she was socialized.

Each individual's frame of mind is reflected in his or her conversational style. Researchers will tell you that some women develop a conversational style that leans toward developing intimacy and nurturing relationships. Many women may use this frame of mind in their negotiations as a means of making a connection with other people and avoiding isolation. Men want intimacy too, but often to a lesser degree.

Some men may tend to approach their negotiations as contests, striving to keep their independence and status, and to avoid failure. Women seek independence and status, but usually to a lesser degree than men.

In short, it's common for men and women to focus on different details and have different perceptions of the same conversation.

In the following pages, I list the INSTANT NEGOTIATOR five steps again. This time I point out how a man's desire for status and a woman's preference for intimacy may affect the way in which both sexes could communicate while negotiating, regardless of their opponent's gender.

Change the way you picture in your mind the stereotypical roles of each gender. Flexible thinking should prevail.

Step 1: Know Your Opponent

Men Need to Know:

- Many women may tend to build rapport best when communicating and receiving a lot of verbal and physical feedback such as facial expressions and gestures.

- Many women focus on keeping intact the relationship with their opponents. They may see value in giving and accepting support. They may prefer to explain how they've shared similar experiences as their opponents.

- Some women may also want confirmation of their concerns rather than hearing only solutions from their opponents.

Women Need to Know:

- Men tend to define themselves by their accomplishments. So they may prefer to talk about their achievements and avoid talking about personal issues that may reveal a weakness.

- A lot of men are goal-oriented and place a strong value on solving problems and reaching goals. As a result they might not understand that some opponents don't want to hear their solutions.

- Some men have a tendency to be competitive in their negotiations. They may talk a lot only to prove their knowledge instead of feeling a need to build rapport.

Step 2: Understand the Challenge

Men Need to Know:

- In personal negotiations, women who talk openly about their problems may be trying to reinforce the relationship. They may also ask a lot of questions in order to develop a connection with an opponent.

- Many women may assume that male opponents should talk openly about their feelings on the issues being negotiated. Some women may mistake a man's reticence as disapproval or disagreement.

- If a woman gives drawn-out answers to questions, it could mean she's verbalizing her thought process and looking for her opponent to address her concerns. This is common for both men and women.

Women Need to Know:

- A lot of men naturally pull away from intimacy and may become evasive if they feel pressured to talk about their feelings in personal negotiations.

- When some men face problems, they may prefer to seek solutions in silence. This could create a barrier for opponents hoping to get their questions answered while trying to understand the challenge.

- Some men may tend to avoid asking a lot of questions for fear they might look unknowledgeable. This could prevent them from fully understanding the needs of their opponents.

Step 3: Introduce New Alternatives

Men Need to Know:

- Many women prefer to negotiate by brainstorming with their opponents. They may have a desire to give advice and direction on how to find solutions.

- When some women give advice on how to make things better, they perceive their advice as a deep personal desire to help, and they expect the opponent to accept the advice graciously.

- For some women, the need for help is not a sign of weakness. And they sometimes pride themselves on offering good solutions.

Women Need to Know:

- Many men prefer to achieve results by themselves. They may reject the notion of brainstorming sessions with their opponents.

- When a man hears advice from a female, he may perceive it as an implication that he is inadequate, and he may become defensive.

- For some men, asking for help is a sign of weakness. But when they realize they need help, seeking help sometimes becomes an act of wisdom.

Step 4: Set the Rules

Men Need to Know:

- Some women may find it unnecessary to set the rules with an assertive request about how they want the negotiation process to go. (Women should be aware of this as well.)

- Sometimes a woman may attempt to justify the reasons for rules she sets, instead of simply setting them and expecting her opponents to follow them. (Women should be aware of this as well.)

- Many women tend to be very intuitive. They may offer clues to the rules they expect, assuming that their opponents are as intuitive and that they will understand the clues.

Women Need to Know:

- When a man is confronted with an indirect question from an opponent, he may perceive the question as a complaint or a threat.

- Some men, while being direct in setting rules, may prefer that their opponents be just as direct.

- A lot of men are much more willing to go along with the rules set by an opponent when they feel respected and appreciated.

Step 5: Go for Agreement

Men Need to Know:

- When seeking an agreement, some women may be so concerned about their opponent's and their own concerns that the substance of the issue may become secondary.

- Many women may think out loud for the purpose of discovering their true inner thoughts. When presenting her alternatives, a woman may "over-communicate" to help convince herself of the benefits.

- Some women may become silent in a negotiation when they lose trust in an opponent or when thinking negative thoughts. So women may interpret a man's silence in the same way.

Women Need to Know:

- Some men become so engrossed in the substance of the issue that they might overlook their opponent's most important needs.

- Some men could consider an opponent's discussion as busy talk and could fail to use the information to more clearly understand what the opponent needs to feel satisfied.

- A lot of men become silent in their negotiations when they're trying to think up solutions to their problems, not necessarily because they disapprove of their opponents.

It's All in the Presentation

At a company Christmas party, a high-level executive named Barbara, a strikingly attractive woman, asked a much younger man named Gary, a mail room intern, to guess her age. When Gary hesitated, Barbara nudged, "Gary, you must have *some* idea."

"I have several *ideas*," Gary replied with a smile. "The problem is that I can't decide whether to make you ten years younger because of your looks, or ten years older because of your charm."

Touché!

Summary

- ☉ Whatever the biological or sociological reasons, women and men often communicate differently. We must understand that differences could exist if we want to negotiate effectively with the opposite sex.

- ☉ Differences in communication styles often create barriers, and they commonly muddle negotiations between women and men.

- ☉ Each person may perceive the other sex from a perspective that has developed from the manner in which he or she was socialized.

- ☉ Change the way you picture in your mind the stereotypical roles of each gender. Flexible thinking should prevail.

CHAPTER ELEVEN

Sales Success Through Negotiation

You're a Negotiator and a Salesperson

If you've ever sold anything, then you negotiated terms that both sides found mutually beneficial. Even if you are not a professional salesperson, chances are you still sell and negotiate on a regular basis.

Have you ever convinced someone to see a movie with you that you liked or to eat at a certain restaurant that you enjoy? People naturally sell themselves and their own ideas to other people.

Selling doesn't always have to involve transferring a product or service. It mostly has to involve persuasion. If you've ever persuaded someone, then you have used the skills of a salesperson.

I make this point because even though this part of the book is designed to help salespeople incorporate the INSTANT NEGOTIATOR system into their businesses, anyone can use this information to sell their ideas or persuade others.

Selling with the INSTANT NEGOTIATOR Five Steps

The INSTANT NEGOTIATOR five-step system is so powerful because it has a universal nature. The five steps not only move you systematically through any type of negotiation to reach satisfaction, they also guide you through the selling process. When you follow this systematic approach to selling, it can lead you to an effectively negotiated, closed sale with the most desirable result—the best price possible for you and a satisfied customer.

Selling and negotiating go hand in hand, yet few sales trainers link the two. Many fail to address the negotiation process as part of closing a sale. In my opinion you can't sell successfully, on a regular basis, unless you know how to negotiate. Sure, you can persuade someone to your way of thinking without negotiating. That may seem like a successful sale. But will the "buyer" follow through and close the deal? Negotiation helps move people to buy whatever you're selling. Consider this example:

Real estate mogul Donald Trump, in his book *The Art of the Deal*, tells a story of how he persuaded someone to his way of thinking. But he still had to negotiate after successfully persuading his opponent. In this case Trump happened to be a buyer, but he was selling his idea to the head of New York retailer Bonwit Teller.

Trump explains that for several years he attempted to convince the management of Bonwit Teller to sell its building on Fifth Avenue in Manhattan. Trump wanted the building and the company's land lease so he could build a new skyscraper. Eventually, the head of Bonwit Teller at the time, John Hanigan, agreed to sell Trump the building and land lease. They also agreed on the price of $25 million. But Hanigan made the deal contingent upon approval by his board of directors.

In reality, Trump hadn't yet secured the purchase because the board could decide not to go through with the deal. Despite his success at selling his idea, Trump hadn't completely closed the deal. He had to continue negotiating on the details of the sale. Ultimately, he negotiated with Hanigan to eliminate the need for the board's approval, and the deal was completed.

The Benefits of Effective Negotiation in the Sales Process

The best salespeople I've ever met all share a common trait. In addition to being likable and believable, they understand negotiation and how to incorporate negotiation skills into the sales process. Making a great sales presentation can help a salesperson make a living, but being able to negotiate differences, to close the sale, is what creates wealth for salespeople.

Negotiation provides three primary benefits in sales:

1. Negotiation increases sales volume.
2. Negotiation achieves the best sales price.
3. Negotiation protects the salesperson's commission.

Take a look at how the following sales scenario demonstrates the benefits of negotiation skills in the sales process:

A saleswoman for an East Coast window manufacturer was selling hurricane-proof windows to a home improvement retailer. Although the retailer was convinced it was a quality product, he wasn't sure the design and appearance would appeal to customers in his market. Therefore, he didn't want to take the risk of purchasing the minimum amount of windows that the manufacturer required.

Knowing that the market had already demonstrated a strong interest in her product, the saleswoman offered to waive the minimum order requirement. She agreed to initially sell her customer a smaller supply of the product, at a discount, to test in his market. In return, she asked the retailer to commit up front to a larger-than-usual bulk purchase in sixty days at full price, but only if the initial supply sold within that time frame.

The saleswoman sold her products and negotiated a deal that satisfied her customer. Her ability to creatively negotiate when the persuasion broke down kept the sale alive and ultimately helped close the deal.

Increasing Sales Volume

Negotiation often comes into play when the salesperson and buyer disagree on a particular issue other than price—when the persuasion breaks down, and the sale is in jeopardy. The retailer in this scenario wasn't convinced that the windows would sell in the marketplace. So the saleswoman negotiated a creative deal that eventually overcame the retailer's objections.

Achieving the Best Price Possible

Knowing that her products would sell in the marketplace, the saleswoman convinced her customer to commit up front to a bulk purchase at full price. Although she offered a discount on the initial supply, she was able to achieve the best price possible on future shipments of her product.

Protecting Commissions

Not only did the saleswoman convince the retailer to pay full price, she also committed him to purchasing a larger-than-usual bulk supply when the initial discounted supply sold. What the saleswoman may have lost by offering an initial discount, she would make up in the larger bulk purchases, thereby protecting her commission.

How the INSTANT NEGOTIATOR Five Steps Close a Sale

You've probably heard of buyer's or seller's remorse. It happens all the time. People feel a sense of panic after they've just sold or purchased something. The panic results when the person isn't positive he or she got the best price. Remorse is most prevalent when people have failed at negotiating a sale effectively—when either party doesn't feel satisfied.

Satisfaction is the key. People can negotiate price and terms, reach an agreement, and somewhere along the line still not feel satisfied.

The same five steps presented earlier, which are designed to satisfy everyone involved in a negotiation, are now presented as a guide for the sales process. They'll help you increase the chances that your prospect will find satisfaction in the deal and ultimately live up to the agreement.

Step 1: Know Your Opponent

Building Business Relationships

The BMW car salesman thought he had his customer pegged. The thirty-year-old man sported a crisp, light-blue dress shirt, dark blue pants, and a gold silk tie. The salesman *knew* that the customer was just like many other "yuppie" types looking to make a statement about his success. And a new BMW could bring the prestige he was looking for.

"Imagine what all your friends will say when they see you driving around in a new BMW. It spells success," said the salesman.

The young man turned to the salesman and simply replied, "Thank you." He left the building without ever buying a new car.

What went wrong? The salesman didn't know that the young man was very wealthy. He was also a devout Christian who practiced modesty and pledged his whole life never to honor possessions over the love of God. The customer was turned off by the salesman's pitch.

Although they could afford the best, he and his family lived modestly. The young man was only looking at luxury cars because his wife had recently given birth to a baby girl. They were searching for a new car the baby would be safest in—one that offered extra safety features not available in less expensive cars. The man was more concerned with protecting his new baby than about showing his friends how financially successful he was.

This is a classic story of the unskilled salesperson failing to get to know his prospect, not identifying the prospect's motives, and losing a sale as a result. He never even got the chance to negotiate because he never had a potential sale.

Too many salespeople either assume all people are buying for the same reasons, or forget that people don't always buy for the sake of ownership. People buy the benefits that products and services offer them.

Each person may find value in a different benefit. In this case the young man was hoping to buy safety and peace of mind, not a luxury car. Had the salesman known this, he could have persuaded the young man that BMW offered the safety features he wanted. The salesman could have negotiated the deal with an advantage—the power of knowing that his opponent harbored a specific, urgent need that he could satisfy.

Recognize that people typically buy the benefits that a product or service offers them.

You can't know what an opponent's needs are until you take the time to build rapport (in sales negotiations the "opponent" is a prospect, buyer, or anyone you're trying to persuade). Good rapport offers your prospects a comfort level that, in turn, encourages them to reveal their true feelings about what they want and their logical reasons for what they believe they need (see Step 1 to review strategies for getting to know your opponent). Building rapport means getting people to like you and, more importantly, to trust you. Obtaining this trust takes a sincere effort on your part. The word "sincere" is the key.

The great self-help guru Dale Carnegie made this point clear in his writings. He explained that people, no matter what their economic class or cultural background, are mostly interested in themselves. When you allow prospects to talk about themselves, you are more likely to gain their favor. One good way to get people to talk is to simply ask questions such as: **"What are your thoughts on this?"** It's often a better selling strategy to know what your prospect is thinking before you begin selling your product.

Asking probing questions within the framework of a cordial conversation, as opposed to an interview, helps uncover a prospect's motives. Questions such as: **"Are you originally from this area?"** or **"What type of work do you do?"** are typical "get to know you" questions that don't seem too intrusive and are a good starting point. Along with creating a friendly atmosphere and being a good listener, asking lighthearted questions sends a message to a prospect that you're genuinely interested in what matters to him or her.

Asking questions also reveals a prospect's circumstances and allows you to qualify her. Some people might not be in a financial position to pay your price. You'll want to identify these circumstances before you spend valuable time moving through all five steps.

Take a sincere interest in your prospect's needs.

Carnegie also wrote about the importance of smiling to make people feel welcome, and he pointed out the value of remembering and using people's names. "A person's name," Carnegie wrote, "is to that person the sweetest and most important sound in any language."

Say your opponent's name during the conversation: **"Joe, I see what you mean,"** or **"I had a similar experience, Jennifer."** People like to hear others say their names—but only in a sincere tone.

In sales, "cold calling" leaves you little opportunity to build rapport with a busy prospect. In this case you may need to grab the attention of the prospect first by offering benefits of your product up front, such as: **"I have a new product that can clean your equipment at half the cost of all the others."** Offering the best possible benefit works in these cases. But remember to avoid selling the product—just sell the benefit. This type of attention grabber opens the door for you to build rapport later on.

These may all seem like common-sense suggestions. But there's more to the big picture. This first INSTANT NEGOTIATOR step gives you an opportunity to closely observe your prospects' emotions, their feelings about specific issues, their body language, and the needs that their questions reveal. This information helps you understand the prospects' motivations, which, in turn, will help you develop a sales negotiation strategy.

Buying Motives

People make buying decisions based on two basic motives: pleasure and pain.

Pleasure: People buy products or services that make them feel joyful, comforted, entertained, loved, prestigious, admired, successful, healthy, competitive, satisfied, etc.

Pain: People buy products or services to help them avoid feeling sad, discontented, anxious, unloved, disliked, financially troubled, unhealthy, unsafe, dissatisfied, etc.

Take the time to identify your prospect's buying motives.

Sometimes a person's motives could conflict when his or her *wants* and *needs* are different. People commonly buy items they *want* but don't *need*. Consider the woman renting an old, run-down, mobile home yet who wore a three-carat diamond ring on her finger. She had saved for years to buy it. The ring was worth more than her home. The woman, raising two children by herself, probably *needed* a larger, safer home. Instead she purchased the ring she *wanted*.

Some people choose to buy based mostly on how they feel, making decisions that follow their emotions. If a prospect appears willing to express his or her emotions, try asking "feeling" questions such as: **"How would you feel if you could reduce your payments by fifteen percent?"** or **"What's your feeling about life insurance investments?"**

Being respectful of emotions in the buying process, you should not ignore an opponent's logical reasoning. People justify their wants with logical reasons. The woman with the large diamond and a mobile home justified her purchase by saying, "It's an investment that won't lose its value, and I can sell it later and recoup my money."

Logic can help close the sale when a person's emotions diminish. If that same woman had feared taking the final step to buy that ring, a salesperson could have said, "You're buying this at such a great price that if you want to sell it later you'll get your money back." That type of logic could lead a buyer to the closing table.

The bottom line with this step is that you want to get to know who you're dealing with—what makes the person tick. You also want them to know that you've taken a sincere interest in them. It encourages prospects to give you an opportunity to sell them something. And it creates an amicable environment in which to negotiate.

Step 2: Understand the Challenge

Identifying the Prospect's Problem and Overcoming Obstacles

Most modern sales techniques incorporate a strategy of solving problems to help make a sale. If you can solve people's problems to their satisfaction, they will usually buy from you. Many prospects don't clearly understand their problems. It's your job to identify the problems and gently point them out to your prospect.

In this step, your questioning changes its focus. During the previous step, while building rapport, you learned "what" or "how" a person feels. In this step, while identifying problems, you want to know "why" a person feels a certain way. The "why" questions should be more direct, seeking responses to specific issues that people usually bring to the forefront themselves during general conversation.

Present "why" questions that could reveal your prospect's problem.

I have a friend who is president of a successful mortgage brokerage firm. When people come to him for home mortgage loans, the first question he asks after building rapport is, "Considering the variety of more beneficial loan programs available, why do you prefer a fixed interest rate?" He certainly knows that most people are not familiar with the variety of loan programs available. He asks the question anyway just to point out the problem—that most people don't know which loan program is best for them. His customers then rely on him to solve that problem. Keep in mind, he didn't create the problem; he simply revealed it with effective questioning.

The proper questions elicit answers that help you understand how you can help your prospect. Make a checklist of questions to ask yourself first. The answers to self-directed questions will help you develop appropriate questions to ask your prospects.

Here are some examples of self-directed questions:

- How much does the person already know about my product or services?
- Do I clearly understand the prospect's motives?
- Is there more than one problem I can identify?
- Have I made any false assumptions about the prospect?
- What are the prospect's expectations?
- What are my price limits, and what are his or her price limits?
- Is the prospect using a competitor's service?
- What are his or her feelings about my competitors?
- Does the prospect understand the differences between what I have to offer and what my competitors offer?

Obviously, there can be no standard checklist of self-directed questions. Each is unique to a salesperson's industry. We suggest you create the checklist over time. Eventually the checklist will help you create effective questions that elicit answers you'll anticipate, and they'll identify problems you already know how to solve.

Make a checklist of questions to ask yourself before you begin questioning your prospect.

A prospect's answers will often reveal obstacles or objections to the potential sale. This gives you an opportunity to solve your own problems before they emerge in the final sales negotiation. Take the story of an assertive high-tech manufacturing manager. His company makes computer chips used in automobiles. He was planning to sell his new boss, the new president of the company, on a strategy of reducing overhead by placing limits on hiring and by purchasing more efficient computer equipment. Before making his presentation, he asked this question: "Why are we meeting over the issue of our production efficiency?"

The president answered, "By all accounts I believe we are understaffed. I hope to increase our employee base by at least ten percent."

Right away, the plant manager knew that his idea of a hiring freeze was already in jeopardy.

Step 3: Introduce New Alternatives

Creating Options and Alternatives that Add Benefits

A lot a stories are written about government inefficiency. The following story made me both laugh and feel frustrated at the same time:

In the 1960s the U.S. and the Soviet Union were scrambling to win the "space race." The National Aeronautics and Space Administration (NASA) reportedly spent millions of dollars researching and developing a special ball-point pen that astronauts could use in their zero-gravity space capsules. Russian cosmonauts faced the same problem, but they chose to use a pencil.

This story suggests that solutions to some problems are often simple— and are certainly less costly than extravagant ideas. The simple, common-sense approach is the first step in creating beneficial options for your sales prospect. Once you've identified your prospect's problem, you'll want to create solutions in which the prospect will see a benefit. Often, you don't have to stretch your imagination too far. Remind yourself to look at common-sense solutions first. They will be easiest for the prospect to understand and accept.

Breaking each problem down to its smallest components helps you see the problem more clearly and can lead you to simple solutions—but only if a simple solution exists.

An example of breaking a problem down is the story of Pat, an advertising executive who found an ingenious way to beat his competition. During his attempt to sell billboard advertising to a restaurant, he learned that his prospect was considering purchasing advertising from a competitor whose price was less. But the competitor's billboard site was less desirable.

Although the price for Pat's billboard was three hundred dollars more per month, the number of cars that drove past the site was double—almost ten thousand more cars per day. He broke the restaurant's options down to a basic component by saying, "The difference is less than ten dollars per day. Are you willing to cut your visibility in half for such an insignificant savings? If our billboard, which is visible to ten thousand more potential customers per day, brings in only two customers per week, you've earned money on your investment."

When the solution is not that simple, your creativity comes into play. The Reverend Robert Schuller tells the story of how young F. W. Woolworth left his retail job to open a store of his own. Just before Woolworth's grand opening, a competitor down the street placed an ad in the newspaper that read, "We have been in business for 50 years!" Woolworth needed a creative solution to this problem. The next week he placed his own ad. It read, "We've been in business for only one week—all of our merchandise is brand new." Woolworth went on to great financial success.

The Power of "What If"

Asking "what if" or implication questions of your prospect can help with creative problem solving. Implying possible alternatives can generate more information that helps feed your creative thinking process. Furthermore, "what if "questions often encourage your prospect to brainstorm with you for solutions.

A computer software salesperson selling database programs could ask, "What if a more efficient customer contact system could help increase referral business?" A wholesale paper supplier could ask a greeting-card shop owner, "How would a diversified product line help you capture a larger customer base?" Since these are not "yes" or "no" questions, but instead require dialogue, you can test your prospect's opinion on possible solutions. Remember that you're not offering definite solutions at this time. You're just testing the waters.

When you create solutions for your prospect to consider, you need to examine the benefits of each solution or option to make sure they all meet your prospect's needs. Each option should operate in a flexible framework. You should be able to take pieces of one option and and connect them to another option. Your goal is to have a mix of alternatives that can be intermingled so you can ultimately build the most beneficial solutions. Here's an example:

A computer salesperson is creating options for a large law firm that needs an entirely new computer networking system. The firm's partners have several problems with a new computer system. The cost is too high for them to pay all at once; they don't have any employees who are skilled in computer network systems; they are concerned that advancing technology will result in their system becoming obsolete too quickly; and they need the system up and running as soon as possible to keep up with an increasing workload and competition. The salesperson can offer the following options:

1. The law firm can opt for a computer lease plan that requires a smaller monthly payment.
2. The law firm can trade in the computers later for updated technology.
3. The computer company can offer training to employees at a discount.
4. The computer company can offer to use its own skilled employees to transfer data from the old system to the new system during weekend hours.
5. The computer company can offer to sell the firm's old computers on consignment.

In the realm of negotiating, this step of introducing new alternatives adds value for both sides involved. In essence, it expands the pie so both sides can take a piece they find valuable. In the sales forum, you go one step further. You structure a mix of options that will entice your prospect to buy. Offering your opponent options that add value certainly increases the likelihood that you'll close the sale.

Step 4: Set the Rules

Set Limits for Prospects to Follow

The most powerful way to establish control of the sales process is to set the rules. It's amazing to me how few people use this tool to gain an edge in either the sales or the negotiation process. By setting rules, you commit your prospect up front to following *your* rules. What's more powerful than that?

Does setting the rules always work? Maybe not every time. But you should at least try it—because when it does work, your chances of closing a deal increase dramatically.

Setting rules provides six fundamental benefits to salespeople. In each benefit, there's an example of what someone might say to set the rules. Keep in mind that the rules are unique to each sale, and you make up whatever rules you want to help make a successful sale.

1. Setting rules sets the stage for the sales presentation: **"These services are not exactly what you asked for, but pay close attention to the additional benefits and I think you'll find them more valuable."**

2. Setting rules obtains a preliminary commitment from the prospect: **"If these options don't meet your goals, it's important that you let me know so we can work together to find the right solution."**

3. Setting rules can stop objections before they arise: **"The price for this service is higher than the amount you first mentioned. But we need to review the added benefits to see if they outweigh the cost."**

4. Setting the rules reinforces the quality of your products or services: **"You already know how fast our delivery system is, so I know you'll take that into account when considering our latest products."**

5. Setting rules gives you power to ask for additional sales up front: **"We're giving you the absolute best wholesale price. All I ask is that you allow us to supply you with these additional products…"**

6. Setting rules transfers perceived power from your prospect to you: **"My company knows how to service your needs. Once you've looked at my competitors, we can sit down and discuss how we can offer better service than anyone."**

It's amazing what you can accomplish by taking the liberty of setting the rules!

Don't underestimate the power of setting the rules before a sales presentation.

STEP 5: Go for Agreement

Presenting Alternatives and Closing the Sale

Earlier we discussed how people buy things based on logic and emotions. Logic gives them the interest to consider buying. Emotions drive people to go through with the purchase. Emotions create the desire in people to experience the benefits of whatever they're buying. As a salesperson, you must be able to tap into those emotions. Make people feel that desire and help them visualize the benefits.

Your presentation skills should stir a prospect's emotions to the point of creating enough desire for him or her to buy. Your presentation should also include logical reasons that justify the emotions.

Stir a prospect's emotions to the point of creating enough desire for him or her to buy.

Let's take a look at some presentation rules:

Validation

People don't rely solely on what salespeople promise about a product or service as a reason for buying. They typically want proof. Your presentation should validate the product and give the buyer a chance to test the product, hear testimonials, or read newspaper or magazine articles expressing favorable opinions. You can also show comparisons in the form of visual aids, charts, graphs, and pictures. Physical proof grabs the attention of the prospect and helps him or her understand the benefits more clearly.

Speak Easy

I was amazed to hear that research on the topic of people's fears suggests that on the list of things people fear most, death was number two. What was number one? Public speaking! Relatively few people enjoy it.

How can you have a successful career if you cannot speak with ease before a group of potential customers? You can't!

The best way to eliminate the fear of speaking is simply to do it often. Join a civic or business organization that requires you to speak in front of an audience regularly. Don't think you need to become a champion motivational speaker. You simply need to eliminate the fear so that you don't hesitate to speak authoritatively when making a presentation.

Being nervous is a normal part of speaking in front of people. Expert speakers use that nervous tension as a positive. They turn those "butterflies" into a positive force that peps up their energy and enthusiasm during the presentation. If you're not enthusiastic about what you're offering, how can you expect the prospect to have any interest at all? Show enthusiasm!

Enthusiasm does not mean talking so fast that nobody can understand you. Speak in a deliberate, methodical way without being mechanical or contrived. Work on pronouncing your words clearly and using voice inflection to express your feelings about the products you're selling. Avoid mumbling and stumbling and verbal pauses like "uh" or "um." Consistent practice will help you avoid these problems. You can practice by reading out loud for thirty minutes every day. Read as if you're speaking: experiment by changing your voice inflections and pace. Keep in mind that your voice is a selling and negotiating instrument. You should practice learning how to use the instrument to get the most out of it.

Demonstrate the Product or Service

Salespeople demonstrate their products as a method of introducing their functions. A product's functions can certainly grab the attention of prospects, especially if it's a new and interesting item. Persuading them that a func-

tion provides a benefit to them entices people to buy. Consider this sample
outline for your demonstrations of products or services:

- **Assume the prospect knows nothing.** Salespeople who gain extensive knowledge of their products sometimes unknowingly omit important information from their demonstrations. They assume the
  prospects already know the seemingly insignificant details when, in
  fact, those small points may help someone grasp the concept. As you
  move through the demonstration, you should gauge the prospect's
  knowledge and adapt the demonstration accordingly.

- **Simplify the product.** People don't want to pay for something that's
  going to make life difficult for them. Whatever your product is, show
  how simple it is for the prospect to use. If your product is not simple
  to use, you'd better find some powerful benefit for making someone's
  life more difficult.

- **Put the prospect to work.** You want to keep your prospect's attention. The best way is to have them help you with the demonstration.
  Ask the prospect to try the product or repeat to you their understanding of the service. Don't make it difficult. You don't want to embarrass
  the person.

- **Ask questions.** Throughout the entire demonstration, you should peri-
  odically ask questions and seek affirmative answers. You want the person to get into the habit of answering "yes" and responding in a positive manner. That way they'll be more likely to say yes when you
  negotiate on the final sale.

- **Bridge the function and the benefits.** The most important part of
  the demonstration is defining how the function of the product offers
  an advantage to the prospect. Use phrases like: **"You will find this
  of great value, Mr. Prospect, because..."** or **"This benefits you for
  several reasons..."**

- **Close the deal.** If you don't close the sale, you haven't negotiated well.
  If you don't negotiate well, you don't eat well, either. How do you close
  the deal? You simply ask the prospect to accept what you're offering.
  If you believe that your product or service will help someone, that mes-

sage should come across to the prospect. But people don't usually reach into their wallets unless asked.

Inevitably some people will reject your request for a commitment to buy. They will usually have a reason, some objection that is holding them back. This is where negotiation plays a major role.

Test the Objection

Salespeople face three primary types of objections: real objections, false objections, and underlying objections.

Real objections: A prospect may have legitimate concerns about the product or service. He or she will usually point these out and explain the disadvantages of whatever it is you're selling.

False objections: Prospects use false objections simply to avoid the decision-making process. They have no specific concerns about what you're selling; they're just not willing to make a buying decision.

Underlying objections: These objections are the most difficult to understand because the prospect hides them from you. There's a reason the prospect won't close the deal, but he or she is reluctant to reveal the reasons.

Tips for Handling Objections

Empathize. Let the person know that you understand his or her objection. Explain that other people have felt the same way—even that you've felt the same way in some of your purchases. Remind the prospect that you're a consumer, too, and that you have to make similar buying decisions.

Turn the objection into a question. To address the prospect's negative feelings behind the objection, you need to find out what's causing the feeling. You need to understand the "why" of the objection. Turn the objection into a question rather than making an argument to prove the prospect wrong. Take a look at the following example.

Prospect: "Our company can't afford to pay that kind of advertising cost."

Salesperson: "Is it the initial cost that you're questioning, or are you looking at the long-term cost compared with the benefit?"

This type of response implies that the "objection" is really just a question waiting to be answered.

Create choices. As a salesperson, you probably hear the same objections over and over again. Therefore, you should already have in place a list of options for your prospects. Once you learn what's motivating the objection, you can offer the appropriate choices. If the objection is related to price, give pricing options for the prospect to choose from, or explain why it's an excellent value. If the objection relates to the delivery time of a product, offer a variety of ways it can be delivered with different schedules: **"We can ship it overnight with company A for this price, or in two days with company B for this price, or with a local trucking company for that price…"** The goal is to allow your opponent to make choices instead of making excuses.

Verify the goal. If your prospect is really looking to buy but has legitimate objections, then you should be able to verify the prospect's goal with definitive statements. For example, you could say: **"If these options meet your needs, I'll prepare to have them shipped in a suitable time frame."** Any prospect who would say, "Well…I still don't know…" might have false or underlying objections. In that case you'll need to refer back to "Turn the objection into a question" and get to the bottom of the objection.

Ask for the sale. Once you think you've effectively handled the objection, ask your prospect to agree to the sale. Don't wait for the prospect to think up more objections.

Some of the information in "Sales Success Through Negotiation" may seem redundant because a lot of it is the same as the INSTANT NEGOTIATOR five steps. But that's the point. It merges the sales and negotiation processes, increasing your chances not only of making the sale, but of negotiating the best price, terms, and benefits for both you and your customer.

There's one major difference between using the five steps strictly for negotiating and using them for sales. In negotiation, although you always strive for a win/win result, you accept a win/lose result if you're winning over a difficult opponent. During the sales process, if you don't satisfy your opponent, you can't make a sale.

Summary

- ⏱ Recognize that people typically buy the benefits that a product or service offers them.

- ⏱ Take a sincere interest in your prospect's needs.

- ⏱ Take the time to identify your prospect's buying motives.

- ⏱ Present "why" questions that could reveal your prospect's concern.

- ⏱ Make a checklist of questions to ask yourself before you begin questioning your prospect.

- ⏱ Offering your opponent options to consider and value to take from the deal increases your chances of closing the sale.

- ⏱ Don't underestimate the power of setting the rules before making a sales presentation.

- ⏱ Stir a prospect's emotions to the point of creating enough desire for him or her to buy.

Now You Know It—Use It

The Future Is Now!

In the Star Wars movie *The Empire Strikes Back*, the character Yoda says to his Jedi warrior subordinates, "Try? There is no try. There is only do or not do." That's the way you should look at negotiation.

You have the INSTANT NEGOTIATOR skills in your hands. Put them to use. Practice them and perfect them—begin improving your life.

Although not everything is negotiable, you'd be surprised to know how much *is*. Following is a list of low-risk deals that you can practice with. They can either get you into the habit of negotiating or help you enhance the negotiation skills you already use. Most of all, have fun with your new skills!

- Go to a garage sale and negotiate over anything.

- Have a garage sale yourself, and place yourself in a position to make a deal.

- Buy a new suit and get an accessory like a tie or belt thrown in for free.

- Buy flowers for your significant other and negotiate for extra flowers in the bouquet.

- Call a hotel and make a deal for the best room rate.

- Call an airline and let them know you're shopping the Internet for the best fare.

- Convince your spouse to cook you a meal you love.

- Negotiate with a family member over which television show to watch at home or which music to listen to in the car.

- Make a deal over the price of getting your car detailed. Get the carpets steam-cleaned at no extra cost.

- Call your finance company and request a lower interest rate on your auto loan.

- Ask for a massage at half-price to see if you would want to get massages on a regular basis.

- Negotiate with your banker for a higher interest rate on a certificate of deposit.

Each day for the next week, write down all the negotiable situations you find yourself in. Keep a journal of how you move through the INSTANT NEGOTIATOR five steps and what the end result is. Ask yourself if you could have made a better deal for yourself. This practice will help you develop the INSTANT NEGOTIATOR mind-set. Eventually, negotiating will become second nature to you. And you'll sharpen your skills over time.

In a book titled *Think and Grow Rich, A Black Choice*, authors Dennis Kimbro and Napoleon Hill describe an amazing study of how people choose to live their lives. The book tells of a prominent psychologist who posed this question to three thousand people: "What do you have to live for?" Ninety-four percent of the people who responded said **they had no definite purpose for living**. According to Kimbro and Hill, these people were ". . . simply enduring the present while they waited for the future."

Are you just enduring life, waiting for the future? Well, your future has already arrived. Your future is whatever you want it to be at this moment. All you have to do is take the negotiating skills you've learned and use them. Control your destiny. And remember: *What you achieve in life is in direct proportion to how well you negotiate.*